Powers and Pitfalls of Facebook, Twitter, and Instagram

C. P. Kumar
Reiki Healer
Roorkee - 247667, India

Copyright © 2023 C. P. Kumar

All rights reserved.

No part of this book may be reproduced or transmitted in any form or by any means, electronic or mechanical, including photocopying, recording, or by any information storage and retrieval system, without permission in writing from the author.

Disclaimer

While every effort has been made to ensure the accuracy and completeness of the content in this book, the author cannot guarantee that the information contained herein is error-free, up-to-date, or suitable for every individual circumstance.

The author shall not be held liable or responsible for any errors or omissions in the content of the book, nor for any damages, or losses that may arise from any actions taken based upon the suggestions or contents presented in the book.

Readers are advised to use their own judgment and discretion in applying the information provided in this book, and to consult with qualified professionals before taking any action based on the contents of this book. The author disclaims any and all liability or responsibility for any actions taken or not taken based on the information contained in this book.

DEDICATION

To all those who seek to understand the intricate web of human connection and communication in the digital age.

This book is dedicated to the curious minds, the critical thinkers, and the tireless seekers of knowledge who recognize the immense power and potential that platforms like Facebook, Twitter, and Instagram hold. Through the exploration of their rise, evolution, and impact, may we unravel the complexities and uncover the truths that shape our online interactions.

To the users who navigate the algorithmic labyrinth, may these pages illuminate the pathways and pitfalls that govern our digital experiences. May you find insights to empower you to make informed decisions and forge genuine connections in a world where algorithms often dictate the course of our interactions.

To the guardians of privacy and advocates for responsible technology, may this book shed light on the intricacies of privacy concerns, content moderation challenges, and the dark underbelly of fake news, disinformation, and harassment. Your efforts in fostering a safer online environment are commendable, and this work stands as a testament to your endeavors.

To the influencers and content creators who shape the cultural zeitgeist, may these chapters offer a balanced perspective on the influence, impact, and commercialization of social media. In a landscape where authenticity battles with filters and body image struggles with reality, may this book encourage introspection and dialogue.

To the policymakers, lawmakers, and regulators who grapple with the task of balancing free speech and responsibility, may these words provide valuable insights into the role of social media in political discourse, activism, diplomacy, and the news landscape. Your decisions shape the future of digital communication, and this book aims to contribute to informed deliberation.

To the dreamers and visionaries who envision a future where social media serves as a force for good, may this book inspire forward-thinking solutions and a collective effort to address the challenges that lie ahead.

With admiration for the human spirit's relentless pursuit of understanding, connection, and progress,

C. P. Kumar

CONTENTS

Copyright 2

Disclaimer 3

DEDICATION 4

PREFACE 8

Chapter 1.   The Rise of Social Media 10

Chapter 2.   The Evolution of Facebook................16

Chapter 3.   The Twitter Phenomenon...................20

Chapter 4.   Instagram 24

Chapter 5.   Algorithmic Influence........................28

Chapter 6.   Privacy Concerns on Facebook...........33

Chapter 7.   Facebook's Content Moderation Challenge 37

Chapter 8.   The Dark Side of Facebook 42

Chapter 9.   Twitter Trolls and Online Harassment................46

Chapter 10.   Twitter and Free Speech....................51

Chapter 11.   Twitter Wars and Cancel Culture......................55

Chapter 12.   Instagram Influencers and the Culture of Influence 60

Chapter 13.   Instagram and the Commercialization of Social Media 65

Chapter 14.   Instagram vs. Reality........................70

Chapter 15. Body Image and Instagram.................................74

Chapter 16. The Social Impact of Facebook..........................79

Chapter 17. Facebook's Role in Political Discourse 84

Chapter 18. Twitter's Role in Activism and Social Movements
....89

Chapter 19. Twitter Diplomacy 95

Chapter 20. Twitter and the News Landscape 101

Chapter 21. Election Interference and Social Media
Manipulation..105

Chapter 22. The Influencer Economy 110

Chapter 23. Instagram's Impact on Cultural Trends and
Globalization...114

Chapter 24. Regulating Social Media 120

PREFACE

In an age defined by connectivity, we find ourselves immersed in a digital landscape shaped by the remarkable evolution of social media platforms. Facebook, Twitter, and Instagram have emerged as virtual crossroads where billions converge, sharing thoughts, images, and experiences in unprecedented ways. These platforms, once heralded as conduits of unity and expression, now stand as both beacons of innovation and cautionary tales of unforeseen consequences.

This book seeks to unravel the intricate tapestry of powers and pitfalls that these platforms embody. It is a comprehensive exploration of the impact, influence, and implications of social media in our lives. As we journey through these pages, we'll traverse the historical milestones and transformative shifts that have shaped the rise of social media, leading to the ubiquitous presence of Facebook, Twitter, and Instagram.

Our exploration begins by tracing the origins and subsequent evolution of each platform. From humble beginnings, they have grown into cultural phenomena, each with its distinct identity and role in our digital society. We'll investigate the algorithmic underpinnings that shape the content we encounter, alongside the profound privacy concerns that have surfaced in an era of unprecedented data sharing.

The book delves deep into the challenges faced by Facebook in curating its vast content landscape and the intricate struggles against disinformation and manipulation. Likewise, Twitter's dynamic landscape is dissected, from its role in fostering public discourse to the complexities of managing online harassment and the ever-present tension between free speech and accountability.

Instagram's visual revolution takes us on a journey through the world of influencers and filters, exploring the impact of its image-centric culture on authenticity, mental health, and commercialization. The intersection of these platforms with political discourse, activism, and even diplomacy forms a crucial part of our exploration, underscoring the far-reaching consequences of a tweet or a post in an interconnected world.

Throughout this book, we invite you to ponder the intricate balance between the potential for positive change and the dangers of unintended harm. We aim to foster a deeper understanding of the forces at play in the realm of social media, empowering readers to navigate this digital landscape with discernment and responsibility.

As we embark on this expedition through the Powers and Pitfalls of Facebook, Twitter, and Instagram, we encourage you to approach each chapter with an open mind and a critical lens. In doing so, we hope to equip you with the insights necessary to engage with these platforms as informed and conscientious participants in our digital age.

Let the journey begin.

C. P. Kumar
Reiki Healer
Former Scientist 'G', National Institute of Hydrology
Roorkee - 247667, India
E-mail: cpkumar@yahoo.com
Web: https://www.angelfire.com/nh/cpkumar/virgo.html

Introduction

In the modern digital age, the emergence and proliferation of social media platforms have transformed the way people communicate, share information, and interact with each other. Facebook, Twitter, and Instagram are three iconic platforms that have played pivotal roles in this revolution. This article delves into the remarkable rise of social media, examining its powers in connecting people globally while also exploring the potential pitfalls that come with the immense influence of these platforms.

The Evolution of Social Media

Social media's journey can be traced back to the early days of the internet when online bulletin boards and forums provided individuals with a space to exchange ideas and connect. As technology advanced, platforms like Six Degrees, considered the first social media site, laid the foundation for more interactive experiences. However, it was Facebook, founded by Mark Zuckerberg in 2004, that truly revolutionized social networking by introducing features like user profiles, friend connections, and photo sharing.

1. Facebook: The Pioneer of Social Networking

Facebook's exponential growth marked a turning point in the digital landscape. The platform's user-friendly interface and innovative features attracted millions, quickly transforming it from a college-specific network to a global phenomenon. Through the power of algorithms, Facebook's News Feed personalized content for each user, enhancing engagement and extending its influence beyond personal connections to encompass news, entertainment, and even political discourse.

2. Twitter: Redefining Microblogging and Real-Time Information

In 2006, Twitter introduced a novel concept - microblogging - allowing users to share their thoughts, news, and updates in bite-sized 140-character posts, known as tweets. The original character limit was 140 characters which was increased to 280 in 2017 and now the limit has been pushed to 4,000 for Twitter Blue subscribers. The platform's real-time nature made it an invaluable tool for sharing live events, sparking conversations, and even influencing public opinion. Hashtags emerged as a way to categorize and trend topics, amplifying the global impact of social movements and viral trends.

3. Instagram: The Visual Revolution

While Facebook and Twitter focused on text-based content, Instagram, launched in 2010, harnessed the power of visuals. By enabling users to share photos and short videos, Instagram tapped into the innate human desire for visual storytelling. Its filters and editing tools allowed anyone to become a digital artist, contributing to the rise of influencers and the culture of aesthetic self-presentation.

Powers of Social Media

The rise of these platforms brought forth a multitude of powers that have reshaped society, culture, and communication dynamics.

1. Global Connectivity and Cross-Cultural Exchange

Social media transcends geographical barriers, enabling individuals from diverse backgrounds to connect, share experiences, and bridge cultural gaps. Facebook's "friends" model, Twitter's follower system, and Instagram's visual appeal foster connections that span continents, contributing to a more interconnected world.

2. Amplification of Voices and Causes

Never before have individuals had such a potent platform for amplifying their voices and advocating for social causes. Social media's viral nature allows information to spread rapidly, galvanizing movements and mobilizing communities for change. Movements like #BlackLivesMatter and #MeToo gained traction and sparked global conversations through these platforms.

3. Empowerment and Entrepreneurship

The rise of influencers and online entrepreneurs underscores the empowerment potential of social media. Content creators can build personal brands, share expertise, and even monetize their platforms. Instagram, with its emphasis on visual aesthetics, has given rise to a new generation of artists, photographers, and fashion enthusiasts who have transformed their passions into profitable ventures.

Pitfalls of Social Media

While the powers of social media are undeniable, they are accompanied by a range of pitfalls that raise significant societal concerns.

1. Information Overload and Misinformation

The sheer volume of content on social media can lead to information overload, making it challenging to discern credible sources from misinformation. Echo chambers and filter bubbles exacerbate the issue, reinforcing existing beliefs and hindering critical thinking. An echo chamber is a self-reinforcing environment where individuals are exposed primarily to information and opinions that align with their existing beliefs, reinforcing their perspectives and limiting exposure to diverse viewpoints. A filter bubble is a personalized online environment in which individuals are presented with content that algorithms predict they will like, creating a limited and skewed view of the world by filtering out dissenting or unfamiliar perspectives. The viral spread of fake news and conspiracy theories on these platforms has raised alarm about their impact on public discourse and democratic processes.

2. Erosion of Privacy and Data Exploitation

The convenience of social media often comes at the cost of privacy. Users' personal data is collected, analyzed, and monetized by platforms, advertisers, and third parties. High-profile data breaches and controversies, such as the Cambridge Analytica scandal involving Facebook, have highlighted the potential for exploitation and manipulation of user information.

3. Mental Health and Online Harassment

The constant exposure to curated, idealized images on platforms like Instagram can contribute to feelings of inadequacy and low self-esteem. Moreover, the anonymity afforded by social media can lead to cyberbullying, harassment, and the spread of hate speech. The pressure to garner likes and followers has raised concerns about the impact of these platforms on mental health, particularly among young users.

Navigating the Future

As society continues to grapple with the powers and pitfalls of social media, it becomes crucial to find a balance that maximizes the benefits while mitigating the risks.

1. Digital Literacy and Critical Thinking

Promoting digital literacy and critical thinking is essential in the age of information overload. Education initiatives can empower users to evaluate sources, identify misinformation, and engage in informed discussions. By equipping individuals with the skills to navigate the online landscape, we can foster a more discerning and responsible online community.

2. Ethical Use and Regulation

To address concerns about privacy, data exploitation, and content moderation, regulatory frameworks must evolve. Stricter guidelines for data collection and sharing, as well as transparency in algorithms, can help ensure ethical practices. Collaboration between governments, tech companies, and civil society is essential to create a balanced digital ecosystem.

Social media platforms can take proactive steps to promote positive online behaviors. Implementing robust anti-harassment measures, providing mental health resources, and curbing the spread of false information through algorithmic adjustments can contribute to a healthier digital environment.

Conclusion

The rise of social media, exemplified by Facebook, Twitter, and Instagram, has ushered in an era of unprecedented connectivity, empowerment, and influence. These platforms have the power to shape narratives, mobilize movements, and amplify voices on a global scale. However, the pitfalls, from misinformation to privacy concerns, underscore the need for a thoughtful and balanced approach to their use. As we navigate the complex landscape of social media, it is imperative to harness its powers while safeguarding against its potential pitfalls, ensuring a digital world that fosters connectivity, empowerment, and responsible discourse.

Introduction

In an era defined by the rapid advancement of technology, the emergence of social media platforms has revolutionized the way we connect, communicate, and share information. Among these platforms, Facebook stands as a trailblazer, captivating billions of users worldwide since its inception. This article delves into the multifaceted evolution of Facebook, tracing its journey from a college dormitory project to a global powerhouse, while also addressing the inherent powers and pitfalls that have shaped its trajectory.

The Genesis

The story of Facebook began in 2003 when a Harvard University student, Mark Zuckerberg, embarked on a quest to create a digital platform that would facilitate interaction and connectivity among students on campus. The initial iteration, known as "Facemash," allowed users to compare the attractiveness of their peers. While this concept raised ethical concerns and was swiftly taken down, it laid the foundation for what would soon become Facebook.

Birth of a Social Network

In February 2004, Zuckerberg, along with his college roommates, Andrew McCollum, Eduardo Saverin, Chris Hughes, and Dustin Moskovitz, launched "Thefacebook." Exclusively catering to Harvard students initially, the platform gained immense popularity, leading to its expansion to other Ivy League universities and subsequently, to universities across the United States and Canada. The fundamental concept of connecting individuals based on their educational institutions marked the first step in Facebook's evolution.

From Campus to the World

Recognizing the potential beyond educational institutions, Facebook opened its doors to the general public in September 2006. This pivotal move ignited rapid global expansion, propelling the platform to international prominence. Users across the world could now create profiles, share updates, and establish connections, fostering a sense of interconnectedness that transcended geographical boundaries.

The Social Media Ecosystem

As Facebook continued to gain momentum, its evolution extended beyond the confines of a mere social networking platform. The company embarked on a series of strategic acquisitions, such as Instagram in 2012 and WhatsApp in 2014. These acquisitions not only expanded Facebook's user base but also diversified its offerings, solidifying its presence in various facets of the digital landscape.

Innovation remained at the core of Facebook's evolution. Introduction of the News Feed feature in 2006 transformed how users consumed content, while the "Like" button became a universal symbol of approval. The evolution of the platform's interface and functionalities was a testament to its adaptability and responsiveness to user preferences.

Connecting a Fragmented World

As Facebook's user base swelled into billions, it became a potent tool for social interaction, information dissemination, and even activism. The platform played a pivotal role in raising awareness about social issues, facilitating grassroots movements, and connecting like-minded individuals across the globe. During the Arab Spring uprisings, Facebook emerged as a catalyst for organizing protests and galvanizing change.

However, this newfound power was not devoid of pitfalls. The dissemination of misinformation, echo chambers amplifying divisive ideologies, and the spread of "fake news" underscored the darker side of Facebook's influence. The platform's role in the propagation of misinformation during critical events like elections raised questions about its ethical responsibilities and the need for content regulation.

Monetizing Connectivity

Facebook's evolution was intrinsically tied to its business model, which heavily relied on targeted advertising fueled by user data. The platform's ability to gather user information and tailor advertisements based on individual preferences revolutionized the advertising industry. While this personalized approach yielded substantial profits, it also ignited debates about user privacy and the ethical implications of data collection and usage.

Navigating Choppy Waters

As Facebook's influence continued to expand, so did concerns regarding user privacy. High-profile data breaches and controversies, such as the Cambridge Analytica scandal in 2018, exposed the extent to which user data could be exploited for political and commercial gain. These incidents prompted regulatory bodies worldwide to scrutinize Facebook's practices, leading to calls for greater transparency and accountability.

The Metaverse Beckons

Mark Zuckerberg's vision for Facebook extended beyond its current form. He articulated a vision of a "metaverse" – an interconnected virtual space where users could interact, work, and play. The metaverse is a collective virtual shared space, merging physical and digital realities, where users can interact, socialize, and engage with digital environments and assets. This ambitious concept represents a potential next phase in Facebook's evolution, blurring the lines between the digital and physical worlds. However, it also raises profound questions about the implications for privacy, autonomy, and societal structures.

Conclusion

The evolution of Facebook is a testament to the dynamic interplay between technological innovation, societal dynamics, and economic imperatives. From its humble beginnings in a college dorm room to its current status as a global juggernaut, Facebook's journey has been marked by unprecedented growth, transformative impact, and a fair share of challenges.

As the social media giant continues to shape and be shaped by the world around it, a crucial question looms: How will Facebook's evolution influence the future of human connectivity, information dissemination, and societal progress? Only time will reveal the full extent of Facebook's powers and pitfalls, but its journey remains an integral chapter in the ever-evolving narrative of digital transformation.

Introduction

In the ever-evolving landscape of social media, few platforms have captured the essence of real-time communication and information dissemination quite like Twitter. With its iconic 280-character limit and an incessant flow of tweets, Twitter has emerged as a cultural and societal phenomenon, shaping conversations, influencing politics, and connecting people across the globe. In this article, we delve into the powers and pitfalls of the Twitter phenomenon, exploring its impact on communication, activism, marketing, and the broader social fabric.

Unraveling the Twitter Landscape

The Twitter phenomenon can be best understood by dissecting its key elements and the role it plays in modern digital society. This microblogging platform, founded in 2006, quickly rose to prominence with its unique focus on concise and immediate communication. With its blue bird logo, Twitter encourages users to "tweet" their thoughts, updates, and opinions in 280 characters or less. This bite-sized format lends itself to quick sharing, enabling real-time reactions and engagement.

The Power of Hashtags

One of Twitter's most impactful contributions to the social media landscape is the concept of hashtags. These simple, yet powerful, tools enable users to categorize and follow specific topics, creating a virtual web of interconnected conversations. Hashtags have birthed viral trends, propelled social movements, and even sparked revolutions. From the #BlackLivesMatter to #MeToo, hashtags have facilitated the mobilization of masses, amplifying voices that might have otherwise been unheard.

The Politician's Pulpit

Twitter's reach extends beyond personal interactions; it has transformed the way political figures engage with the public. The platform provides a direct channel for politicians to communicate with their constituents, share policy updates, and even express personal opinions. This unfiltered access, however, can lead to both transparency and controversy. Politicians' unscripted tweets have sparked diplomatic tensions, policy debates, and even contributed to shifts in public opinion. The Trump presidency's use of Twitter exemplified how a world leader could wield the platform as both a powerful tool and a potential pitfall.

Amplifying Activism

Social activism has found a formidable ally in Twitter. Movements advocating for social justice, environmental change, and human rights have harnessed the platform's ability to connect like-minded individuals across the globe. The speed at which information spreads on Twitter enables activists to rally support, organize events, and shed light on injustices. However, this power can also lead to the spread of misinformation, diluting the impact of genuine causes.

Information Onslaught

The rapid-fire nature of Twitter's content delivery can be both exhilarating and overwhelming. The constant stream of tweets from friends, celebrities, brands, and news outlets can create a sense of information overload. This inundation raises questions about the quality and accuracy of the information being consumed. Discerning between reliable sources and sensationalism becomes crucial, as the line between news and noise blurs.

Building Brands in 280 Characters

Businesses have recognized the marketing potential inherent in Twitter's succinct format. Brands can showcase their personalities, launch products, and engage directly with customers in real time. The platform's viral nature means that a well-crafted tweet can spread like wildfire, instantly boosting brand visibility. However, the brevity of tweets also demands a unique approach to storytelling and messaging, where every character counts.

Celebrities in the Spotlight

For celebrities, Twitter offers a direct avenue to interact with fans, share personal updates, and even address controversies. While this direct engagement can foster a sense of intimacy, it also exposes celebrities to immediate criticism and backlash. A single ill-conceived tweet can tarnish reputations, leading to public relations nightmares. The line between a relatable online presence and an invasive spotlight becomes increasingly thin.

The Dark Side

While Twitter facilitates connection, it also exposes users to the darker aspects of online behavior. Trolling, cyberbullying, and harassment thrive in the anonymity of the internet, and Twitter is no exception. The platform's structure, with limited character counts, can sometimes lead to misinterpretation and heated debates. Echo chambers can form, reinforcing existing beliefs and limiting exposure to diverse perspectives.

Censorship and Free Speech

The balance between fostering open dialogue and curbing harmful content places Twitter in a complex position. The platform's decisions regarding content moderation and censorship have drawn intense scrutiny. While policing hate speech and misinformation is essential, these efforts can inadvertently stifle free expression. Striking the right balance between maintaining a safe environment and upholding free speech principles remains an ongoing challenge.

Conclusion

The Twitter phenomenon is a multifaceted and constantly evolving entity that wields immense power to shape narratives, influence opinions, and drive change. Its ability to connect, mobilize, and inform is undeniable, yet it is not without its pitfalls. As society continues to grapple with the impact of social media, platforms like Twitter serve as both mirrors reflecting our collective thoughts and laboratories for testing the boundaries of human interaction. Navigating the Twittersphere requires a keen awareness of its powers and pitfalls, harnessing its potential while mitigating its risks. As we move forward in this digital age, the Twitter phenomenon stands as a testament to the profound influence of social media on our lives.

Introduction

In the realm of social media, few platforms have left as indelible a mark as Instagram. With its inception in 2010, Instagram swiftly transformed the way we interacted with images and visual content. In this age of digital communication, where pictures speak volumes and attention spans grow shorter, Instagram's visual prowess has not only revolutionized how we share our lives but has also ushered in a new era of social connection, creativity, and marketing. As part of the discourse on the powers and pitfalls of social media giants like Facebook, Twitter, and Instagram, it is imperative to delve into the unique impact of Instagram and its role as a visual revolution.

The Birth of a Visual Epoch

Instagram, founded by Kevin Systrom and Mike Krieger, emerged at a juncture where smartphones were becoming ubiquitous and photography was no longer the exclusive domain of professionals. The platform's fundamental premise was simple yet transformative: empower users to capture, edit, and share images effortlessly. This simplicity was instrumental in propelling Instagram's meteoric rise, as it catered to the inherent human inclination to communicate through visuals.

Visual Storytelling

Human beings have communicated through visuals since time immemorial, from cave paintings to hieroglyphics. Instagram tapped into this primal form of communication, allowing individuals from diverse cultures and linguistic backgrounds to connect through images. The platform became a canvas for personal expression, where users could share their life's moments, experiences, and emotions, transcending language barriers. This visual storytelling aspect fostered a sense of intimacy and authenticity that set Instagram apart from its text-centric counterparts.

Catalyst for Creativity

Instagram's filters and editing tools democratized the art of photography, enabling anyone with a smartphone to produce visually appealing and artistic images. This democratization of creativity marked a paradigm shift, challenging conventional notions of who could be considered an artist or a photographer. The platform empowered users to experiment with colors, compositions, and perspectives, leading to the emergence of a vibrant global community of amateur photographers.

Influence on Visual Aesthetics

The rise of Instagram introduced new aesthetic norms and trends, shaping how individuals perceive and present themselves and their surroundings. The platform's emphasis on curated feeds and visually cohesive profiles incentivized users to refine their visual identities. This quest for a visually appealing grid led to the popularization of certain aesthetics, such as minimalism, vintage filters, and vibrant color palettes. Consequently, Instagram's influence extended beyond the digital realm, impacting fashion, interior design, and even urban planning.

The Social Media Celebrity Phenomenon

Instagram played an instrumental role in birthing the era of the "social media influencer." Individuals with a knack for visual content and a unique personal brand leveraged the platform to amass large followings, transcending geographical boundaries. These influencers wielded significant power to shape opinions, consumer preferences, and even social norms. However, this newfound influence also brought to light ethical concerns, as issues of authenticity, sponsored content, and the blurring line between advertising and personal endorsement emerged.

A Force in Marketing and E-commerce

Instagram's visual appeal didn't go unnoticed by businesses and marketers. The platform swiftly evolved into a potent marketing tool, enabling brands to showcase products and engage with audiences in innovative ways. The introduction of features such as shoppable posts and Instagram Checkout revolutionized e-commerce, facilitating seamless transactions within the app. Shoppable posts and Instagram Checkout refer to features on the Instagram that allow users to directly purchase products showcased in posts, turning the platform into an e-commerce hub. While this offered convenience to users, it also entrenched Instagram deeper into the realms of consumerism, raising questions about materialism and the commodification of lifestyles.

Fostering Community and Activism

Beyond its commercial implications, Instagram became a powerful tool for social and political movements. The visual nature of the platform enabled activists to share compelling images and stories, sparking global conversations and mobilizing support for various causes. The use of hashtags to consolidate conversations allowed disparate voices to unite under a common banner, exemplified by movements like #BlackLivesMatter and #MeToo. Nevertheless, the platform's efficacy in driving meaningful change is a subject of ongoing debate, as online activism often intersects with complex real-world challenges.

Navigating the Pitfalls

Amid its myriad strengths, Instagram is not exempt from the pitfalls that plague the broader social media landscape. The platform's emphasis on image-based validation has contributed to a culture of comparison, leading to issues of low self-esteem, body image concerns, and a propensity for seeking external validation. The rise of "FOMO" (Fear of Missing Out) and the pressure to curate an idealized online persona have also raised questions about the authenticity of digital interactions.

Conclusion

Instagram's journey from a modest photo-sharing app to a global visual phenomenon underscores its transformative impact on social media and contemporary culture. The platform's ability to forge connections, amplify voices, and reshape aesthetic norms has ushered in a visual revolution that continues to evolve. As we navigate the powers and pitfalls of digital behemoths like Facebook, Twitter, and Instagram, it is imperative to recognize the nuanced ways in which each platform shapes our lives, perceptions, and interactions. Instagram, with its visual allure and societal influence, stands as a testament to the enduring power of images in an increasingly connected world.

Introduction

In the ever-evolving digital landscape, social media platforms have become powerful tools that shape our daily lives, influence our thoughts, and even impact global events. Facebook, Twitter, and Instagram, three giants of the social media realm, have significantly transformed how we communicate, connect, and consume information. Central to their functioning are intricate algorithms that govern what content we see, share, and engage with. This article delves into the powers and pitfalls of these algorithms, exploring their influence on user behavior, content dissemination, and societal dynamics.

The Algorithmic Paradigm Shift

In the early days of social media, chronological timelines dominated the user experience. However, as these platforms expanded and user-generated content skyrocketed, it became impractical to display all posts in real-time. This led to the rise of algorithms – complex sets of rules and calculations designed to curate and personalize users' feeds. The aim was to enhance user engagement and create more meaningful interactions.

The Power of Personalization

Social media algorithms operate on a fundamental principle: personalization. They analyze a user's past behavior, preferences, and interactions to predict what content they are most likely to engage with. By showcasing relevant posts and filtering out less relevant ones, algorithms aim to capture and maintain users' attention.

This power of personalization, while enhancing user experience, comes with a caveat. The algorithms create echo chambers, reinforcing users' existing beliefs and perspectives. This phenomenon, known as the "filter bubble," can limit exposure to diverse opinions, leading to polarization and an insular online environment.

Content is King

Algorithmic content prioritization dictates the visibility of posts in users' feeds. Engagement metrics such as likes, comments, and shares play a significant role in determining the popularity of a post. Consequently, posts with higher engagement are more likely to be shown to a broader audience.

For content creators and businesses, understanding these algorithms is crucial. Crafting content that resonates with the algorithms can lead to increased reach and engagement. However, this pursuit of algorithmic approval can sometimes compromise the authenticity and originality of content, as creators may tailor their posts to fit the algorithms' criteria rather than their true creative vision.

Viral Velocity

The allure of going viral on social media is undeniable. Algorithms play a pivotal role in this phenomenon, as they identify and amplify content with rapid engagement growth. A single like or share can trigger the algorithm's attention, propelling the content to a wider audience.

While viral content can lead to fame and exposure, it also comes with risks. The algorithms prioritize immediate engagement over long-term value, often favoring sensationalism and clickbait. This emphasis on virality incentivizes content that generates strong reactions, sometimes at the expense of accuracy or ethical considerations.

The Dark Side of Algorithms

The same algorithms that strive to personalize content also inadvertently enable the spread of misinformation. By tailoring content to individual preferences, algorithms can expose users to false or biased information that reinforces their existing beliefs. This has significant implications for societal discourse, as misinformation can easily permeate echo chambers and undermine informed decision-making.

Moreover, malicious actors exploit algorithmic vulnerabilities to manipulate public opinion. The proliferation of fake accounts, bots, and coordinated campaigns can artificially boost engagement metrics, giving a false impression of content's popularity. This manipulation of algorithms poses a substantial challenge to platforms' efforts to maintain a healthy information ecosystem.

The Feedback Loop

User engagement serves as a feedback mechanism that informs algorithmic adjustments. When users interact with specific types of content, algorithms take notice and adapt their recommendations accordingly. This feedback loop perpetuates user behavior, as the algorithms continually refine their understanding of individual preferences.

However, this cycle can lead to a homogenized feed that limits exposure to diverse content. Users might find themselves trapped in a loop of similar posts, stifling the potential for serendipitous discovery and intellectual growth.

Strategies for Navigating Algorithms

1. Diversify Your Feed: **Actively seek out content that challenges your perspectives. Engage with a variety of topics and creators to avoid the filter bubble's limiting effects.**

2. Critical Consumption: **Practice media literacy by fact-checking information before sharing it. Be cautious of sensationalist or clickbait content designed to exploit algorithmic virality.**

3. Mindful Interaction: **Recognize that engagement contributes to the content you see. Prioritize meaningful interactions over mindless scrolling or impulsive reactions.**

4. Platform Settings: **Familiarize yourself with platform settings that allow you to customize your feed's content. Adjust privacy and notification settings to regain control over your online experience.**

5. Algorithmic Transparency: **Advocate for greater transparency from social media platforms regarding algorithmic functioning. Holding platforms accountable can lead to more responsible algorithmic practices.**

Conclusion

The powers and pitfalls of Facebook, Twitter, and Instagram's algorithms are undeniably transformative.

While they enhance user experience, foster connections, and amplify voices, they also raise complex ethical and societal concerns. As we navigate the digital landscape, it is imperative to strike a balance between embracing algorithmic personalization and actively countering its potential drawbacks. By understanding and critically engaging with these algorithms, users can harness their influence while fostering a healthier and more diverse online ecosystem.

Introduction

In an era marked by the digital transformation of communication and social interaction, Facebook stands as a pioneer and a powerhouse. Alongside Twitter and Instagram, it has redefined the way we connect, share, and consume information. The trio has undeniably reshaped the dynamics of personal and societal interaction. However, as these platforms continue to evolve, the powers they bestow upon users are accompanied by a range of pitfalls, particularly when it comes to privacy. This article delves into the privacy concerns surrounding Facebook, shedding light on the multifaceted challenges users and society face while navigating its complex landscape.

The Digital Age of Connection and Surveillance

Facebook's inception in 2004 introduced a groundbreaking concept: the ability to connect and interact with friends, family, and even strangers on a global scale. As the user base grew exponentially, so did its influence, leading to the emergence of the broader category of social media. However, this digital revolution came with a trade-off - the exchange of personal information for connectivity.

Data Monetization

One of the foremost concerns surrounding Facebook revolves around its business model: the monetization of user data. Users often overlook the fact that the platform operates primarily by collecting and analyzing their personal information. This data is then leveraged to target ads with unprecedented precision, allowing advertisers to tailor their messages to specific demographics, behaviors, and interests. While this can enhance the user experience by delivering relevant content, it raises concerns about the extent to which personal information is being exploited for financial gain.

Cambridge Analytica and the Specter of Manipulation

The Cambridge Analytica scandal of 2018 served as a watershed moment in the discourse on privacy and manipulation. It revealed how Facebook data was harvested without explicit user consent to create psychometric profiles (assessments or measurements of an individual's psychological traits, characteristics, abilities, and behaviors), which were then employed to target and influence political opinions during major elections. This incident not only highlighted the potential for the platform to be weaponized against democratic processes but also underscored the vulnerability of user data to unauthorized access.

User-generated Content

Facebook encourages users to share their thoughts, photos, and experiences, fostering a sense of community and self-expression. However, the issue of content ownership and control looms large. While users retain copyright over their content, they grant Facebook a wide-ranging license to use, adapt, and distribute their posts. This has led to concerns about the platform's ownership of the narratives users create and the potential misuse of shared content beyond the user's intent.

Perils of Oversharing and Location Tracking

The immediacy and ease of sharing personal experiences on Facebook can inadvertently lead to oversharing. The desire for likes, comments, and validation can drive users to divulge sensitive information, from personal addresses to vacation plans. Additionally, the platform's location-tracking features raise questions about the potential for misuse, both by advertisers seeking location-based targeting and by individuals with malicious intent.

Algorithmic Echo Chambers and Polarization

Facebook's algorithms play a pivotal role in curating the content users see on their feeds. While intended to enhance user experience by showing relevant content, these algorithms can inadvertently create echo chambers that reinforce existing beliefs and viewpoints. This has been linked to the rise of online polarization and the spread of misinformation, as users are exposed to a limited range of perspectives.

The Illusion of Privacy

The line between public and private information on Facebook can often be blurry. Users may believe their posts are visible only to their chosen audience, but frequent changes to privacy settings and the platform's intricate sharing options can lead to unintended exposure. This illusion of privacy can result in sensitive information becoming widely accessible, highlighting the need for constant vigilance and user education.

Third-party Apps and Data Sharing

While Facebook itself collects vast amounts of user data, the platform's ecosystem extends to third-party apps that often request access to users' accounts. This interconnectivity raises concerns about data sharing practices, as some apps may gain access to personal information beyond what users intended to share. The potential for data breaches through these third-party avenues poses a significant risk to user privacy.

Conclusion

The powers and pitfalls of Facebook are inextricably linked, forming a complex and ever-evolving landscape. Its ability to connect individuals across the globe, share diverse narratives, and mobilize social causes is undeniable. However, these powers come hand in hand with the potential erosion of privacy, data exploitation, and the amplification of societal divisions. As users, regulators, and society grapple with the far-reaching implications of this digital behemoth, it is imperative to strike a balance between harnessing its potential and safeguarding the privacy and autonomy of individuals. Only through thoughtful dialogue, informed decision-making, and proactive measures can we hope to navigate the intricate web of Facebook's powers and pitfalls.

Introduction

The emergence of social media platforms has transformed the way we communicate, connect, and share information. Among these platforms, Facebook has played a pioneering role, enabling billions of users to engage with each other across the globe. As a hub for diverse content, from personal updates to news articles, Facebook has brought both immense opportunities and daunting challenges to the forefront. One of the most pressing challenges that Facebook has faced is the complex task of content moderation.

Understanding Content Moderation

Content moderation, in essence, refers to the process of monitoring and managing user-generated content on digital platforms to ensure that it complies with community guidelines, legal standards, and ethical norms. The rise of social media has exponentially increased the volume of user-generated content, making effective moderation a critical component in maintaining a safe and welcoming online environment. Facebook, with its massive user base and wide-ranging content types, confronts an especially intricate content moderation challenge.

The Scale of Facebook's Challenge

With over 2.99 billion monthly active users (as of July 2023), Facebook stands as the largest social media platform in the world. The platform's users share an astounding array of content daily – from personal photos and status updates to news articles, videos, memes, and more. The sheer scale and diversity of this content make moderation a formidable task. Ensuring that each piece of content aligns with the platform's guidelines and filters out harmful or inappropriate material requires an intricate blend of human intervention and technological innovation.

The Role of Humans and AI

Facebook employs a combination of human moderators and artificial intelligence (AI) algorithms to sift through the massive influx of content. Human moderators review flagged content, make decisions based on community guidelines, and handle complex cases that require nuanced judgment. AI, on the other hand, assists by identifying patterns, keywords, and potential violations at a rapid pace. The collaboration between human moderators and AI is essential to maintaining a balance between accuracy and efficiency.

However, this approach is not without its challenges. The rapid pace of content creation and the potential for bias in AI algorithms pose ongoing difficulties. Striking the right equilibrium between the capabilities of AI and the expertise of human moderators remains an ongoing process.

Navigating Complex Content

The content shared on Facebook spans a wide spectrum – from innocuous and lighthearted to controversial and disturbing. Moderators face the arduous task of distinguishing between legitimate expressions of opinion and hate speech, misinformation, graphic violence, and other forms of harmful content. Straddling the line between safeguarding freedom of expression and preventing the spread of harm requires a nuanced and sensitive approach.

The Nuances of Context and Culture

Cultural diversity and linguistic nuances further complicate the content moderation challenge. What might be considered acceptable humor in one culture could be deeply offensive in another. Understanding context, cultural sensitivities, and language intricacies is pivotal in avoiding undue censorship while still ensuring a safe online environment.

The Struggle Against Misinformation

Misinformation and fake news have emerged as rampant concerns across social media platforms, and Facebook is no exception. False information spreads rapidly, often cloaked in sensationalism and appealing narratives. The platform's content moderation efforts extend to combating the dissemination of misinformation, which has the potential to influence public opinion, incite violence, and undermine trust in credible sources.

The Cat and Mouse Game

The battle against content that violates Facebook's guidelines is akin to a cat and mouse game. As the platform evolves its moderation strategies, malicious actors find innovative ways to circumvent them. Strategies such as clickbait, cloaking (a deceptive practice where the content presented to Facebook's review system or bots is different from what is shown to actual users), and image manipulation challenge Facebook's ability to maintain a safe online space. This constant evolution necessitates ongoing updates and adaptations to content moderation practices.

The Toll on Moderators' Well-being

The responsibility of content moderation falls heavily on the shoulders of human moderators. These individuals, often working behind the scenes, are exposed to an onslaught of disturbing and distressing content on a daily basis. The toll of repeatedly viewing graphic violence, hate speech, and other harmful material can have significant repercussions on their mental health and well-being. Facebook and other platforms are increasingly recognizing the importance of providing adequate support and resources to these essential workers.

Transparency and Accountability

Addressing the content moderation challenge requires a delicate balance between user privacy and transparency. Facebook has faced scrutiny for its handling of user data and content, prompting calls for greater transparency in moderation processes. Users have a right to understand how their data is being used and how content decisions are made. Striving for transparency and clear communication can foster greater trust between the platform and its users.

The Road Ahead

Facebook's content moderation challenge is a dynamic and evolving endeavor. As the platform continues to grow and adapt, it must consistently refine its moderation strategies, leverage technological advancements, and prioritize the well-being of both users and moderators. Striking the right balance between freedom of expression and preventing harm remains a complex puzzle that Facebook, along with other social media giants, must navigate in the years to come.

41

Introduction

The digital age has brought about a paradigm shift in the way we communicate and access information. Social media platforms like Facebook, Twitter, and Instagram have emerged as powerful tools, shaping opinions, connecting people, and revolutionizing information dissemination. However, with great power comes great responsibility, and the rise of fake news and disinformation on these platforms has cast a shadow on their potential benefits. In this article, we delve into the dark side of Facebook, exploring how fake news and disinformation have become pervasive issues with far-reaching consequences.

The Viral Web of Deception

Fake news, a term that was relatively obscure a decade ago, has become a buzzword in contemporary discourse. Facebook, with its massive user base and algorithm-driven content distribution, plays a central role in the rapid spread of fake news. But what exactly constitutes fake news? At its core, fake news refers to deliberately false or misleading information presented as factual news. The digital landscape, characterized by user-generated content and the echo chamber effect, is fertile ground for the proliferation of such deceptive narratives.

The Facebook Factor

Facebook's algorithms are designed to maximize user engagement, often leading to the amplification of sensationalist and emotionally charged content. This algorithmic design inadvertently aids the spread of fake news. The more a piece of content is shared, liked, or commented on, the more prominently it appears on users' feeds, creating a feedback loop that rewards sensationalism over accuracy.

Echo chambers, another consequence of algorithmic content curation, further exacerbate the problem. Users are often exposed to content that aligns with their existing beliefs and opinions, reinforcing their perspectives while shutting out diverse viewpoints. This isolation can make users more susceptible to fake news that aligns with their biases, as critical thinking takes a back seat in a reinforcing cycle of misinformation.

The Manipulation Game

Beyond individual users, larger entities have recognized the potential of Facebook as a tool for mass manipulation. Disinformation campaigns, orchestrated by state actors, interest groups, or malicious actors, exploit the platform's reach to disseminate false narratives on a global scale. These campaigns often target sensitive topics like elections, public health crises, and social issues, aiming to influence public opinion and sow discord.

One infamous example is the alleged Russian interference in the 2016 United States presidential election. Russian operatives utilized Facebook to create and promote divisive content, exploiting societal fault lines and amplifying existing tensions. The consequences of such disinformation campaigns are profound, eroding trust in institutions, undermining democratic processes, and fostering an environment of uncertainty.

The Human Element

While Facebook's algorithms play a significant role in the spread of fake news, the susceptibility of human psychology cannot be overlooked. Cognitive biases, such as confirmation bias and the illusory truth effect, make individuals more prone to accepting and sharing information that aligns with their preconceived notions or that they've encountered repeatedly. Confirmation bias is the tendency to favor, interpret, or seek out information that confirms preexisting beliefs or opinions. Illusory truth effect is the phenomenon where people are more likely to believe false information to be true after encountering it repeatedly. This innate human tendency is exploited by fake news creators who craft narratives designed to resonate with specific groups.

Moreover, the emotional appeal of fake news often bypasses critical thinking. Stories that evoke strong emotions, whether fear, anger, or empathy, are more likely to be shared without scrutiny. This emotional manipulation is a potent weapon in the arsenal of fake news purveyors, as it compels individuals to amplify their messages unwittingly.

Facebook's Response

In response to mounting criticism, Facebook has taken measures to combat the spread of fake news and disinformation. Fact-checking partnerships with independent organizations aim to label or reduce the visibility of false content. However, the efficacy of these efforts remains debatable, as the sheer volume of content makes comprehensive fact-checking a daunting task.

Algorithm adjustments, too, have been implemented to prioritize credible sources and reduce the virality of false information. Yet, striking a balance between curbing misinformation and preserving free expression is a complex challenge. Overly aggressive algorithmic changes could inadvertently stifle legitimate discourse.

The Role of User Education and Media Literacy

While platform-level interventions are crucial, empowering users with the skills to critically evaluate information is equally important. Media literacy, the ability to assess and analyze media content, is a potent defense against the lure of fake news. Educating users about the tactics used by fake news creators, teaching them how to fact-check, and encouraging skepticism can help inoculate individuals against manipulation.

Conclusion

Facebook, Twitter, and Instagram have undeniably transformed the way we communicate, connecting people across the globe and facilitating the exchange of ideas. However, the dark side of these platforms cannot be ignored. The rampant spread of fake news and disinformation on Facebook poses a significant threat to informed democratic discourse, public health, and social cohesion. Addressing this issue requires a multifaceted approach that combines responsible platform design, vigilant fact-checking, algorithmic adjustments, and widespread media literacy education. Only by acknowledging and combating the dark side of Facebook can we hope to fully harness its potential while mitigating its pitfalls.

Introduction

In an era dominated by digital connectivity and virtual interactions, social media platforms have emerged as powerful tools that shape opinions, foster connections, and drive conversations on a global scale. Facebook, Twitter, and Instagram, among others, have transformed the way we communicate and share information. While these platforms offer unprecedented opportunities for networking, self-expression, and social engagement, they also come with their fair share of challenges and pitfalls. One of the most pervasive and troubling issues plaguing these platforms is the rampant prevalence of Twitter trolls and online harassment.

The Promise and Peril of Social Media

At its inception, social media held the promise of a digital utopia, where people from diverse backgrounds could connect, exchange ideas, and participate in meaningful discussions. Facebook, Twitter, and Instagram quickly rose to prominence, enabling users to engage with a vast audience, build personal brands, and even influence public discourse. However, alongside the positive aspects, a darker side emerged—one that thrives on anonymity, hostility, and malicious intent.

The Rise of Twitter Trolls

Twitter, with its concise format and real-time interactions, has become a breeding ground for a particular breed of internet denizen known as trolls. Twitter trolls are individuals who deliberately post inflammatory, offensive, or provocative content with the intention of inciting emotional responses from others. These provocateurs often hide behind pseudonyms or anonymous accounts, allowing them to spread negativity without facing real-world consequences. The anonymous nature of Twitter encourages trolling behavior, as it shields individuals from accountability for their actions.

Understanding Online Harassment

Online harassment encompasses a range of harmful behaviors that target individuals or groups with the intent to intimidate, humiliate, or degrade. From cyberbullying to doxxing, the tactics used by harassers are varied and can have devastating psychological and emotional effects on victims. Social media platforms amplify the reach of such harassment, making it possible for even a single malicious user to inflict widespread harm.

Cyberbullying and Psychological Impact: Cyberbullying involves using digital platforms to harass, threaten, or ridicule others. The relative anonymity of the internet emboldens perpetrators to engage in behavior they might shy away from in face-to-face interactions. The psychological toll on victims can be severe, leading to anxiety, depression, and even suicidal thoughts.

Doxxing and Real-World Consequences: Doxxing is the act of revealing someone's personal information, such as their address, phone number, or workplace, with malicious intent. This can lead to real-world consequences, including stalking, harassment, and physical harm. Social media platforms often inadvertently facilitate doxxing by allowing sensitive information to be shared easily.

: Social media provides a platform for hate speech and discriminatory content that targets individuals based on their race, gender, religion, or other protected characteristics. This not only perpetuates harmful stereotypes but can also lead to the marginalization and exclusion of vulnerable groups.

The Role of Platforms

As Twitter, Facebook, and Instagram grew in popularity, they faced increasing pressure to address the issue of online harassment and trolling. These platforms implemented content moderation policies and tools aimed at curbing harmful behavior. However, the effectiveness of these measures has often been questioned, with critics arguing that inconsistent enforcement and false positives/negatives remain significant challenges.

Algorithmic Bias and Echo Chambers: The algorithms that power social media platforms can inadvertently amplify harmful content by promoting sensationalist or provocative posts. This can lead to the formation of echo chambers—environments where users are only exposed to information that aligns with their existing beliefs, reinforcing harmful ideologies.

Balancing Free Speech and Safety: Social media platforms often grapple with the tension between promoting free speech and ensuring user safety. While it's crucial to uphold the principle of free expression, it becomes problematic when that expression turns into harassment or hate speech. Striking the right balance is a complex and ongoing challenge.

Reporting Mechanisms and User Empowerment: **Many platforms offer reporting mechanisms that allow users to flag abusive or harassing content. While these mechanisms empower users to take action, they can be slow and inadequate in addressing the scale of the problem. Additionally, victims of harassment may be reluctant to report due to fears of retaliation or lack of faith in the platform's response.**

Countering Twitter Trolls and Online Harassment

Effectively addressing the menace of Twitter trolls and online harassment requires a holistic approach that involves the collaboration of platform developers, policymakers, users, and society at large. Here are some potential strategies to mitigate the impact of online harassment:

Improved Moderation Tools: **Social media platforms must continue to invest in advanced moderation tools that can detect and remove harassing content promptly. This includes refining algorithms to identify nuanced forms of harassment and hate speech.**

Transparency and Accountability: **Platforms should provide transparency regarding their content moderation processes and policies. This can help users understand how decisions are made and hold platforms accountable for their actions.**

User Education and Empowerment: **Educating users about online etiquette, responsible digital citizenship, and reporting mechanisms can empower them to protect themselves and others from harassment.**

Stronger Legal Frameworks: **Policymakers should work in tandem with social media companies to establish robust legal frameworks that hold harassers accountable for their** actions. This could involve stricter consequences for cyberbullying, doxxing, and hate speech.

Cultivating a Positive Online Culture: Fostering a culture of empathy, respect, and inclusivity on social media platforms can discourage trolling behavior. When users collectively reject harassment and support one another, the toxic appeal of trolling diminishes.

Conclusion

Facebook, Twitter, and Instagram have revolutionized the way we connect and communicate, but they have also exposed us to the dark underbelly of online interactions. The proliferation of Twitter trolls and online harassment highlights the need for constant vigilance and collaborative efforts to create a safer digital environment. As users, platform developers, and policymakers, it is our collective responsibility to navigate the complexities of social media and harness its potential for positive change while mitigating its pitfalls. Only through a concerted and comprehensive approach can we hope to shape a virtual world that is truly inclusive, respectful, and empowering for all.

Introduction

In the digital age, social media platforms have become powerful tools for communication, expression, and connection. Among the most prominent players in this landscape are Facebook, Twitter, and Instagram. Each platform offers unique features and opportunities, but also presents its own set of challenges and controversies. One key area of debate is the concept of free speech, especially in the context of Twitter. This article delves into the powers and pitfalls of Twitter as it pertains to free speech, exploring its impact on public discourse, the challenges of moderation, and the broader implications for society.

The Role of Twitter in Public Discourse

Twitter, with its character-limited format, has revolutionized how people engage in real-time conversations on a global scale. Its immediacy and succinctness have enabled individuals, organizations, and public figures to share thoughts, news, and opinions rapidly. In this way, Twitter has democratized communication, giving voice to marginalized groups and enabling grassroots movements to gain traction.

However, this openness has also led to challenges. The brevity of tweets can oversimplify complex issues, leading to misunderstandings or misinterpretations. Nuanced debates are often condensed into polarized statements, potentially hindering meaningful dialogue. Moreover, the platform's fast-paced nature can incentivize sensationalism and clickbait, favoring provocative content over thoughtful analysis.

The Paradox of Moderation

Twitter, like other social media platforms, grapples with the delicate balance between free speech and responsible content moderation. On one hand, the platform is committed to maintaining an environment where users can express themselves without fear of censorship. On the other hand, it faces pressure to combat hate speech, misinformation, and harassment that can thrive in such a forum.

The challenge lies in distinguishing between legitimate expression and harmful behavior. Twitter's evolving policies seek to define these boundaries, but the line can be subjective and contentious. Critics argue that aggressive moderation could stifle diverse perspectives, while lax enforcement might enable toxic discourse to flourish.

Combatting Misinformation and Disinformation

Misinformation and disinformation are pervasive on social media, and Twitter is no exception. The platform has taken steps to label, restrict, or remove false content, particularly around topics like elections, public health, and global events. While these efforts are aimed at safeguarding users from deceptive information, they also raise concerns about potential bias in content moderation.

The power to label or remove content brings into question who gets to decide what is true or false. This raises concerns about the concentration of authority and potential political manipulation. Striking the right balance between combating misinformation and preserving diverse viewpoints remains a formidable challenge.

Echo Chambers and Polarization

Twitter's algorithmic timeline, designed to show users content they are likely to engage with, can inadvertently contribute to the formation of echo chambers. Users are exposed to ideas that align with their existing beliefs, reinforcing those viewpoints while limiting exposure to differing perspectives. This phenomenon contributes to societal polarization, where individuals become increasingly entrenched in their own ideological bubbles.

The platform's recommendation algorithms, though intended to enhance user experience, can inadvertently amplify extreme content. This presents a dilemma: How can Twitter encourage healthy discourse without inadvertently promoting harmful or divisive content?

The Role of Public Figures and Accountability

Twitter serves as a platform for public figures, including politicians, celebrities, and thought leaders, to communicate directly with their audience. While this direct interaction can foster a sense of connection and transparency, it also raises questions about accountability. Public figures' tweets can have far-reaching consequences, shaping public opinion and policy debates.

However, the platform's leniency towards public figures can be perceived as a double standard. Some argue that influential individuals are held to a lower standard of behavior, as their tweets might not face the same scrutiny or consequences as those of ordinary users. Striking a balance between allowing open dialogue and holding public figures accountable remains a challenge.

Promoting Healthy Online Dialogue

Recognizing the need for a healthier online environment, Twitter has implemented features to promote constructive dialogue. Features such as threaded replies and prompts encouraging thoughtful replies aim to facilitate more meaningful interactions. However, these features rely on user behavior and may not fully address the root causes of toxic discourse.

Promoting healthy conversations also requires addressing the anonymity that can enable harassment and hate speech. Stricter identity verification measures could deter malicious actors, but they could also compromise user privacy and discourage vulnerable individuals from participating.

Conclusion

Twitter, like its counterparts Facebook and Instagram, wields immense power in shaping public discourse and societal norms. Its commitment to free speech while combating harmful content has generated a dynamic and complex environment. Striking the right balance between fostering diverse expression and maintaining responsible discourse is an ongoing challenge—one with far-reaching implications for democracy, social cohesion, and individual well-being.

As society continues to grapple with the powers and pitfalls of social media platforms, including Twitter, it is crucial to engage in nuanced discussions about the role of these platforms in our lives. The evolution of policies, algorithms, and user behaviors will shape the future of free speech and online interaction, making it imperative to consider the broader impact of these digital spaces on our interconnected world.

Introduction

In the digital age, social media platforms like Facebook, Twitter, and Instagram have revolutionized the way we communicate, share information, and engage with the world. While these platforms offer immense opportunities for connection and expression, they also come with their own set of powers and pitfalls. One of the most prominent phenomena that have emerged in this digital landscape is the concept of "Twitter Wars" and the associated "Cancel Culture." This article delves into the dynamics of Twitter Wars and Cancel Culture, examining the implications of public shaming and the far-reaching consequences in today's society.

The advent of social media has given individuals an unprecedented platform to express their thoughts and opinions, engage with others, and even challenge established norms. Twitter, in particular, with its real-time updates and character-limited posts, has become a breeding ground for intense debates, clashes of ideas, and even full-fledged wars between users. These clashes, often referred to as "Twitter Wars," can escalate quickly, attracting attention from a global audience and resulting in profound consequences for all parties involved.

The Anatomy of Twitter Wars

Twitter Wars typically originate from differences in ideologies, beliefs, or opinions on controversial topics.

They often begin as heated exchanges between users, which then gather momentum as more individuals join the conversation, taking sides and amplifying the conflict. Hashtags, mentions, and retweets turn these wars into trending topics, ensuring that they dominate the platform's discourse for hours, days, or even longer.

One notable feature of Twitter Wars is the brevity of communication. With character limits on tweets, complex ideas are distilled into bite-sized statements, often devoid of nuance. This can lead to misinterpretations, oversimplifications, and a lack of context, fueling the flames of the conflict.

The Rise of Cancel Culture

Twitter Wars frequently intersect with the phenomenon known as Cancel Culture. Cancel Culture involves calling out individuals, often celebrities or public figures, for perceived offensive actions, statements, or beliefs. The goal is to hold these individuals accountable by "canceling" their public support, often resulting in social, professional, and financial repercussions.

Cancel Culture utilizes the power of social media to demand swift action and accountability. Users leverage hashtags and collective outrage to pressure companies, organizations, and institutions to distance themselves from the targeted individuals. This can lead to lost endorsements, job terminations, and public humiliation.

The Power and Pitfalls of Public Shaming

At the heart of both Twitter Wars and Cancel Culture lies the power of public shaming. While public shaming has historical roots, social media has exponentially amplified its reach and impact. The immediate and widespread dissemination of information enables users to hold others accountable like never before. However, this power comes with a dark side.

Pros: Holding the Powerful Accountable

One of the key advantages of public shaming is its potential to hold powerful individuals and entities accountable. In an era where traditional media might hesitate to challenge influential figures, social media allows ordinary citizens to demand transparency, justice, and change. Twitter Wars and Cancel Culture have led to investigations, resignations, and policy shifts in response to public outcry.

Cons: Erosion of Nuance and Due Process

While the intent behind public shaming might be noble, its execution often lacks nuance and due process. The condensed nature of social media posts can oversimplify complex issues, leading to a rush to judgment. In some cases, individuals have been wrongly accused, facing severe consequences for actions they did not commit. The court of public opinion, fueled by trending hashtags, can inadvertently perpetuate injustice.

Consequences of Cancel Culture

The consequences of Cancel Culture can be far-reaching and profound. While the movement has succeeded in holding some individuals accountable for their actions, it has also sparked debates about the appropriateness of the punishment and the potential for redemption. The notion that a single mistake or misguided statement can lead to a person's entire life being upended raises ethical questions about proportionality and the right to rehabilitation.

Additionally, Cancel Culture can have a chilling effect on free speech and open discourse. Fear of backlash might discourage individuals from expressing unpopular opinions or engaging in constructive debates, ultimately limiting the diversity of thought and hindering intellectual progress.

Navigating Twitter Wars and Cancel Culture

In a digital landscape where Twitter Wars and Cancel Culture are prevalent, individuals and organizations must navigate these challenges thoughtfully and responsibly.

Promoting Civil Discourse

Fostering civil discourse is essential to prevent Twitter Wars from spiraling into toxic conflicts. Participants should strive to maintain respect, avoid personal attacks, and engage in productive conversations. Emphasizing empathy and active listening can humanize interactions and lead to a deeper understanding of opposing viewpoints.

Fact-Checking and Contextualization

To counter the pitfalls of public shaming and hastened judgments, fact-checking and contextualization are crucial. Before joining a Twitter War or participating in Cancel Culture, users should verify the accuracy of information and seek to understand the broader context of the situation. This can help prevent the spread of misinformation and unjust consequences.

Balancing Accountability and Redemption

Cancel Culture's focus on accountability should be balanced with the potential for redemption and growth.

People make mistakes, and society should allow for the possibility of learning and change. Instead of seeking to completely obliterate individuals, efforts could be directed toward education, dialogue, and restorative justice.

Conclusion

Twitter Wars and Cancel Culture represent the complex interplay of power and pitfalls on social media platforms like Twitter, Facebook, and Instagram. While these phenomena have empowered individuals to challenge authority and demand justice, they also underscore the need for careful consideration, empathy, and ethical accountability. As we continue to navigate the digital landscape, striking a balance between expressing dissent and fostering understanding will be crucial in shaping a more inclusive and equitable online world.

Introduction

In the age of social media dominance, platforms like Facebook, Twitter, and Instagram have transformed the way we communicate, share information, and shape our perceptions of the world. Among these platforms, Instagram has emerged as a powerful player, redefining the dynamics of influence and cultural impact. This article delves into the phenomenon of Instagram influencers and their role in shaping the culture of influence within the broader context of the powers and pitfalls of social media.

The Rise of Instagram

Instagram, initially launched as a photo-sharing app, has rapidly evolved into a multifaceted platform that enables users to express themselves through visuals, captions, and stories. The emphasis on imagery has created a unique environment where content creators can curate a visually appealing narrative that resonates with their followers. This visual storytelling aspect sets Instagram apart, making it an ideal space for influencers to captivate audiences and build personal brands.

Defining Instagram Influencers

Instagram influencers are individuals who have amassed a substantial and engaged following on the platform. They wield a significant influence over their audience's opinions, choices, and behaviors. These influencers come from diverse backgrounds, ranging from fashion, beauty, fitness, travel, lifestyle, and more. What unites them is their ability to create compelling content that resonates with their followers' aspirations and desires.

The Anatomy of Influence

Authenticity in a Curated World: **One of the key elements that distinguish Instagram influencers is their capacity to maintain authenticity while operating in a world of curated content. Their ability to strike a balance between aspirational and relatable content allows followers to connect on a personal level. By sharing their stories, vulnerabilities, and insights, influencers humanize themselves and bridge the gap between virtual and real-life interactions.**

Fashioning Trends and Redefining Beauty: Instagram influencers have emerged as trendsetters, particularly in the fashion and beauty sectors. Through their posts, they showcase styles, products, and aesthetics, often challenging conventional norms of beauty. This redefinition of beauty standards has played a pivotal role in fostering inclusivity and body positivity, encouraging a more diverse representation of beauty on a global scale.

From #Fitspo to Active Lifestyles: The fitness and wellness industries have witnessed a paradigm shift with the rise of fitness influencers on Instagram. These influencers promote not only physical health but also mental and emotional well-being. By sharing workout routines, healthy recipes, and personal stories of transformation, they inspire followers to adopt healthier lifestyles and prioritize self-care.

Globetrotters and Wanderlust: Travel influencers transport their followers to exotic destinations, sparking wanderlust and shaping travel trends. However, this portrayal of idyllic getaways often raises questions about sustainability and ethical travel practices, highlighting the delicate balance between promoting tourism and preserving cultural and environmental integrity.

The Influencer Economy

Monetization and Brand Collaborations: The influencer economy has created new avenues for individuals to monetize their online presence. Brands recognize the value of influencers in reaching niche audiences authentically. Paid partnerships and sponsored content have become the norm, enabling influencers to turn their passion into a lucrative profession. However, this monetization can sometimes compromise the perceived authenticity of their recommendations.

The Allure and Perils of Fame: As Instagram influencers gain popularity, they step into the realm of online celebrity. The allure of fame brings admiration, but it also exposes them to scrutiny, criticism, and privacy invasion. The pressure to maintain a flawless image and the potential for burnout are constant challenges that influencers navigate in the pursuit of maintaining their digital personas.

The Impact on Mental Health: While influencers inspire and uplift their followers, the pressure to maintain an idealized image can take a toll on their mental health. The pursuit of likes, comments, and engagement can lead to feelings of inadequacy and anxiety. This paradox underscores the need for a more nuanced conversation about the mental health implications of influencer culture.

Ethics, Authenticity, and Transparency: Maintaining authenticity and transparency is a recurring challenge in the influencer landscape. The disclosure of sponsored content, the authenticity of endorsements, and the blurring lines between personal and promotional content raise ethical concerns. Striking the right balance is crucial to preserving the trust between influencers and their followers.

The Changing Dynamics

Micro-Influencers and Niche Communities: **The influencer culture is shifting towards micro-influencers – individuals with smaller but highly engaged followings. These micro-influencers often have a more profound impact on niche communities, fostering genuine connections and conversations. Brands are recognizing the value of these authentic connections and are redirecting their influencer strategies accordingly.**

Video Content and IGTV: **IGTV, short for "Instagram TV," is a feature on the Instagram. It was introduced by Instagram in June 2018 as a way for users to share and discover longer-form video content. IGTV is designed to accommodate videos that are longer than the typical one-minute limit for regular Instagram posts. With the advent of IGTV and the popularity of short video formats, Instagram influencers are adapting their content strategies. Video allows for a more immersive experience, enabling influencers to share longer-form content, tutorials, and behind-the-scenes glimpses. This shift toward video is reshaping the way influencers engage with their audiences.**

Social Responsibility and Advocacy: **Many influencers are leveraging their platforms for social causes and advocacy. From environmental issues to social justice campaigns, influencers are using their reach to raise awareness and drive meaningful change. This transformation from trendsetters to advocates highlights the potential for** influencers to shape cultural conversations beyond consumerism.

Conclusion

Instagram influencers have undeniably reshaped the landscape of influence and cultural impact. Their ability to create, inspire, and drive conversations has turned social media into a dynamic arena for cultural expression. However, with great power comes great responsibility. As influencers continue to shape perceptions and trends, it is imperative to strike a balance between authenticity, ethical considerations, and a genuine commitment to positively influencing the culture they help shape.

In the ever-evolving landscape of social media, Instagram influencers stand as both architects and products of the culture of influence, reflecting the powers and pitfalls of platforms like Facebook, Twitter, and Instagram themselves. As we navigate this new era of digital influence, understanding the intricacies of this culture is essential for both content creators and consumers alike.

Introduction

In today's digital age, social media platforms have transformed the way we connect, communicate, and consume content. Among the leading players in this realm, Instagram stands out as a prominent example of the intersection between personal expression and commercialization. This article delves into the evolution of Instagram and its role in the broader landscape of social media commercialization, exploring its impact on users, businesses, and society at large.

The Rise of Instagram

Since its inception in 2010, Instagram has undergone a remarkable evolution. Initially established as a platform for sharing visual moments and capturing snapshots of life, it has rapidly transformed into a multifaceted tool for personal branding, business promotion, and cultural influence.

Instagram's founders, Kevin Systrom and Mike Krieger, envisioned a platform that would allow users to share their lives through images. However, the platform's acquisition by Facebook in 2012 marked a turning point, setting the stage for its expansion into a global powerhouse. Instagram's integration with Facebook's extensive user base and advertising infrastructure paved the way for its commercialization.

Personal Branding

One of Instagram's most significant contributions to the commercialization of social media is the rise of personal branding. Users have transformed their profiles into curated showcases of their lifestyles, interests, and aspirations. The platform's emphasis on visual storytelling has enabled individuals to cultivate distinct personal brands, blurring the line between the personal and the professional.

Influencers, individuals who amass sizable followings based on their expertise, lifestyle, or aesthetics, have become central figures in Instagram's commercial landscape. These influencers collaborate with brands to promote products, effectively monetizing their online personas. This symbiotic relationship between influencers and businesses has created new avenues for advertising, but it has also sparked debates about authenticity, disclosure, and the blurred lines between content and advertisement.

The Business of Visual Commerce

For businesses, Instagram's visual-centric format offers a unique opportunity to engage with audiences in a captivating manner. The platform's user-friendly interface, coupled with its photo and video sharing capabilities, has enabled brands to showcase products and services in creative ways, fostering a deeper connection with consumers.

Instagram's introduction of features such as shoppable posts and in-app checkout has further accelerated its role in e-commerce. Users can now seamlessly transition from browsing a post to making a purchase, streamlining the consumer journey and transforming the platform into a virtual storefront. This integration of social media and e-commerce has not only generated revenue for Instagram but has also reshaped the way businesses approach online sales.

Challenges and Controversies

While Instagram's commercialization has brought forth numerous opportunities, it has also been accompanied by a range of challenges and controversies. The pursuit of likes, comments, and followers has fueled concerns about mental health and self-esteem, particularly among younger users who are more susceptible to the pressures of online validation.

Additionally, the proliferation of sponsored content and influencer partnerships has prompted discussions about transparency and advertising ethics. Striking a balance between authentic expression and brand collaboration remains a complex task, raising questions about the authenticity of user-generated content and the potential for deceptive marketing practices.

The Cultural Impact

Beyond personal branding and business endeavors, Instagram has played a pivotal role in amplifying cultural trends and social movements. The platform's visual nature has facilitated the rapid dissemination of visual content related to activism, politics, and social causes. From viral hashtags to impactful imagery, Instagram has served as a platform for individuals and communities to raise awareness and mobilize support for various issues.

However, this cultural impact also comes with its own set of challenges. The algorithmic curation of content may lead to filter bubbles and echo chambers, limiting users' exposure to diverse perspectives. The line between meaningful activism and performative gestures can become blurred, raising questions about the depth and authenticity of online social engagement.

Future Prospects

As Instagram continues to evolve, its future trajectory raises important considerations about striking a balance between commercialization and user experience. The platform's ability to innovate and adapt will determine its sustainability in an ever-changing digital landscape.

Enhancing user privacy and data protection while facilitating targeted advertising poses a delicate challenge. Instagram must navigate evolving regulations and user expectations to ensure that its commercial endeavors align with ethical and legal standards.

Furthermore, as user demographics shift and digital behaviors evolve, Instagram's role in shaping cultural norms and commercial trends will remain a subject of intrigue. The platform's potential to drive societal change, both positive and negative, underscores the need for ongoing research and analysis.

Conclusion

Instagram's journey from a simple photo-sharing app to a global commercial powerhouse reflects the broader narrative of social media's commercialization. The platform has redefined personal branding, revolutionized e-commerce, and facilitated cultural conversations. However, it has also grappled with issues related to authenticity, mental health, and ethical advertising practices.

As Instagram continues to navigate the complex interplay between user engagement, business interests, and societal impact, its story serves as a microcosm of the broader powers and pitfalls inherent in the commercialization of social media. Understanding Instagram's evolution provides valuable insights into the ways in which digital platforms shape our lives, influence our decisions, and redefine the boundaries between personal expression and commercial enterprise.

Introduction

In today's digital age, social media platforms have become a ubiquitous part of our lives, shaping how we connect, communicate, and present ourselves to the world. Among these platforms, Instagram stands out as a visual powerhouse, captivating millions with its stunning images and curated feeds. However, beneath the glossy filters and perfectly composed shots lies a complex interplay between authenticity and artifice. This article delves into the dichotomy of "Instagram vs. Reality," exploring how authenticity is portrayed and often distorted through the lens of filters and digital manipulation.

The Allure of Instagram

Instagram, founded in 2010, quickly rose to prominence as a platform that celebrates visual storytelling. It empowers users to share their lives, passions, and creative expressions through a carefully constructed grid of images. The platform's filters, offering an array of effects from vintage to vibrant, allow users to transform mundane moments into captivating visual narratives. The result is an alluring depiction of reality, a world where every coffee cup seems perfectly frothy and sunsets perpetually glow.

The Quest for Authenticity

Amid the polished perfection of Instagram, a yearning for authenticity emerges. Users, once entranced by the glossy facade, begin to seek more genuine connections and representations. This quest for authenticity has led to a growing movement of users sharing unfiltered, unedited images—moments of vulnerability that challenge the curated norm. Hashtags like #NoFilter and #AuthenticityMatters have gained traction, highlighting the desire to peel back the layers of digital enhancement and embrace reality in all its imperfections.

Filters: Enhancing or Distorting Reality?

Filters, once heralded as tools for enhancing images, have come under scrutiny for their potential to distort reality. While filters can add a captivating veneer to a photo, they can also alter skin tones, body shapes, and landscapes in ways that perpetuate unrealistic beauty standards. The pressure to conform to these idealized images has raised concerns about the psychological impact on users, particularly young and impressionable individuals who may develop skewed perceptions of self-worth.

The Psychology of Perception

The interplay between filters and reality taps into the psychology of perception, revealing how easily our minds can be influenced by manipulated images. Research has shown that even subtle alterations to photos can significantly impact how they are perceived, leading to a "Instagramification" of reality. Users, both creators and consumers, must grapple with the cognitive dissonance between the idealized images and the messy, imperfect nature of everyday life.

From Comparison to Connection

While Instagram's curated feeds can foster comparison and envy, they also offer a unique platform for connection and self-expression. Users are now using their profiles to share personal stories of triumph and struggle, breaking down the barriers of picture-perfect portrayal. Influencers, once celebrated solely for their flawless aesthetics, are now praised for their authenticity and willingness to reveal their unfiltered lives. This shift challenges the traditional notions of fame and success on social media.

The Rise of Authentic Influencers

The rise of authentic influencers, who prioritize transparency over perfection, marks a turning point in the Instagram landscape. These influencers share unfiltered images, discuss personal challenges, and use their platform to advocate for body positivity, mental health awareness, and social justice. Their impact extends beyond aesthetics, empowering followers to embrace their true selves and reject unrealistic beauty ideals.

The Role of Brands and Advertisers

As the dynamics of Instagram evolve, brands and advertisers face a conundrum: how to navigate the tension between the allure of filters and the demand for authenticity. While some companies continue to endorse the polished look, others are aligning themselves with authentic influencers whose messages resonate with a more discerning audience. This strategic shift reflects a broader recognition of the changing expectations of consumers and the growing influence of authenticity-driven narratives.

Digital Literacy and Media Literacy

The "Instagram vs. Reality" debate underscores the importance of digital literacy and media literacy in today's interconnected world. Users must develop critical thinking skills to decipher between manipulated images and genuine representations. Moreover, platforms like Instagram have a responsibility to educate users about the potential pitfalls of filters and digital enhancement, promoting a more balanced and realistic approach to self-presentation.

Conclusion

In the era of Instagram, the juxtaposition of authenticity and filters has sparked a profound conversation about identity, perception, and societal norms. The platform's visual allure continues to captivate, but its users are demanding more than just aesthetic gratification. The push for authenticity challenges us to redefine our understanding of beauty, success, and connection in the digital age. As Instagram evolves, so too does our understanding of reality—both the images we project and the narratives we embrace. The interplay between authenticity and filters is a dynamic, ongoing dialogue that reflects the complexities of our modern relationship with social media.

Introduction

In today's digital age, social media platforms like Instagram have become a pervasive part of our lives, offering a platform for individuals to share, connect, and express themselves. With its visually driven content, Instagram has quickly become a space where users showcase their lifestyles, experiences, and, notably, their bodies. While this can foster a sense of community and self-expression, the incessant exposure to carefully curated images has brought to light a concerning issue: the impact of Instagram on body image and mental health. This article delves into the intricate relationship between body image and Instagram, exploring both the empowering potentials and the detrimental pitfalls that this platform presents.

The Allure of Instagram

Instagram's popularity stems from its unique emphasis on visual content. Users share photos and videos that depict various aspects of their lives, from picturesque landscapes to fashionable outfits, and yes, even their bodies. The platform serves as a canvas for individuals to express their identities, document experiences, and share moments of significance. It has become a tool for self-discovery and self-presentation, enabling users to shape and control their online personas.

The Culture of Comparison

As Instagram continues to evolve, a pervasive culture of comparison has emerged. Users are bombarded with carefully curated images of seemingly flawless bodies, perpetuating unrealistic beauty standards. Influencers and celebrities often set these standards, and their polished posts can lead to feelings of inadequacy and self-doubt among users who inevitably compare themselves to these idealized images.

Research has shown that excessive exposure to idealized body images on Instagram can contribute to body dissatisfaction and low self-esteem, particularly among young users. This phenomenon is exacerbated by the platform's "highlight reel" nature, where users predominantly share their best moments. This creates an illusion that others lead perfect lives, leaving viewers feeling as if their own lives don't measure up.

The Feedback Loop

The reward system on Instagram, characterized by likes, comments, and followers, plays a significant role in shaping users' perceptions of themselves and their bodies. Positive feedback can boost self-esteem and body image, while a lack of engagement or negative comments can lead to feelings of rejection and inadequacy.

The pursuit of validation through social media interactions can lead to a cycle of seeking approval for one's appearance. Users may post content primarily to garner likes and comments, rather than for genuine self-expression. This can distort one's relationship with their body, linking self-worth to external validation rather than internal acceptance.

Fear of Missing Out

Instagram's "Fear of Missing Out" (FOMO) phenomenon can further exacerbate body image concerns. As users scroll through their feeds, they may encounter images of friends or influencers engaging in activities or displaying bodies that align with societal ideals. This can evoke feelings of inadequacy and pressure to conform, intensifying body-related insecurities.

Additionally, FOMO-driven behaviors, such as extreme dieting or excessive exercise, can arise from the desire to fit in or be seen as attractive based on societal standards. These behaviors, while motivated by a desire for acceptance, can lead to physical and mental health issues, including disordered eating and body dysmorphia.

Filtering Reality

Instagram's built-in filters and editing tools enable users to enhance their photos, altering aspects like lighting, color, and even body proportions. While these tools can enhance the visual appeal of images, they also contribute to a distorted representation of reality. The line between genuine self-expression and digitally altered perfection becomes increasingly blurred, fostering an environment where authenticity takes a back seat to aesthetic appeal.

The prevalence of edited images can create an unattainable standard of beauty, perpetuating the notion that flaws and imperfections should be hidden. This can lead to feelings of shame and insecurity among users who don't measure up to the digitally altered images they see on their feeds.

Empowerment and Representation

While Instagram's impact on body image has garnered concern, it's important to acknowledge the platform's potential for positive change. Many users, recognizing the power of authenticity, have embraced a counter-narrative. Body-positive influencers and activists use Instagram to promote self-acceptance, diversity, and inclusivity. They showcase bodies of all shapes, sizes, and abilities, challenging the conventional beauty standards perpetuated by mainstream media.

Furthermore, individuals who have struggled with body image issues find solace in sharing their stories on Instagram. The platform's global reach allows for the formation of supportive communities where users can connect, empathize, and inspire each other on their journeys toward self-love and body positivity.

Mindful Consumption

As we navigate the complex relationship between body image and Instagram, it's crucial to adopt strategies that prioritize mental well-being:

Curate Your Feed: Be mindful of the accounts you follow. Unfollow or mute accounts that consistently trigger negative feelings or promote unrealistic beauty standards.

Practice Digital Detox: Allocate specific times for engaging with social media and set boundaries to prevent excessive usage.

Seek Authenticity: Follow accounts that prioritize authenticity and promote body positivity. Surrounding yourself with diverse representations of bodies can contribute to a more realistic perspective.

Embrace Real Moments: Share genuine experiences, both highs and lows, to contribute to a more authentic online environment.

Prioritize Self-Care: Engage in activities that promote self-esteem and self-worth outside of social media. Nurture your physical and mental well-being through exercise, hobbies, and quality time with loved ones.

Conclusion

Instagram's impact on body image and mental health is a multifaceted issue. While the platform can foster a sense of connection, creativity, and empowerment, it also perpetuates harmful beauty ideals and fosters comparison-driven mindsets. The responsibility lies not only with individuals to curate their digital experiences but also with platform developers, influencers, and society at large to promote a more inclusive and empathetic online culture.

As we continue to navigate the powers and pitfalls of social media platforms like Instagram, it's imperative that we prioritize mental health, challenge societal norms, and harness the platform's potential for positive change. By doing so, we can create an online environment that celebrates diversity, authenticity, and the inherent worth of every individual, regardless of their appearance.

Introduction

In the digital age, social media platforms have become integral parts of our lives, transforming the way we communicate, share, and connect with one another. Among these platforms, Facebook stands as a titan, exerting a profound influence on society. Its impact, both positive and negative, has been a subject of fervent debate, shedding light on the powers it bestows and the pitfalls it presents. This article delves into the multifaceted social impact of Facebook, dissecting its role in shaping relationships, amplifying voices, driving societal change, and wrestling with the darker side of digital interactions.

The Power of Connection

Facebook emerged as a revolutionary platform, breaking down geographical barriers and enabling connections across continents. Long-lost friends reunited, families separated by borders found a virtual space to share moments, and cultures intermingled in unprecedented ways. Through its user-friendly interface and diverse tools, Facebook facilitated the sharing of personal stories, photographs, and life updates, fostering a sense of global community.

While Facebook's power to connect is undeniable, it also comes with pitfalls. The allure of virtual connections sometimes overshadows genuine face-to-face interactions, leading to a digital divide in relationships. Over-reliance on online communication has led to concerns about the erosion of genuine social skills, raising questions about the authenticity of the connections formed on the platform.

Amplifying Voices

Facebook provided a megaphone for marginalized voices, allowing individuals to raise awareness about issues close to their hearts. Grassroots movements gained momentum as activists utilized the platform to organize, share information, and galvanize supporters. Social and political change found a new ally in the form of digital activism, with hashtags and viral content driving real-world impact.

However, this amplification of voices also brought forth challenges. The spread of misinformation and echo chambers became more pronounced, as algorithms tailored content to reinforce users' existing beliefs. The viral nature of sensationalist content sometimes overshadowed well-researched information, leading to a society grappling with the veracity of the information it consumes.

Redefining Social Norms

Facebook's introduction of the "like" button transformed the way individuals perceive validation and self-worth. As posts garnered likes and reactions, a new form of social currency emerged. Users began to associate their online popularity with their real-world value, leading to a phenomenon where self-esteem became intricately tied to virtual approval.

This shift has had a profound impact on mental health. The quest for likes and the pressure to present a curated, idealized version of one's life led to the rise of "Facebook envy" and feelings of inadequacy. The platform inadvertently became a breeding ground for comparison and anxiety, prompting discussions about the need for digital detox and a reevaluation of how online interactions affect mental well-being.

The Business of Influence

Facebook redefined advertising and brand promotion, offering businesses an unprecedented platform to reach a vast audience. Influencer culture was born as individuals with large followings leveraged their presence to endorse products and services. The line between personal and promotional content blurred, transforming social interactions into potential marketing strategies.

While this presented opportunities for businesses, it also raised ethical concerns. The authenticity of influencer endorsements came under scrutiny, and the potential for manipulation of public opinion became evident. The algorithm-driven nature of content distribution led to a homogenization of content, overshadowing smaller businesses and stifling diversity in the online marketplace.

Navigating Privacy

Facebook's growth came hand in hand with debates about user privacy. The platform's ability to collect and analyze vast amounts of personal data raised concerns about surveillance, data breaches, and the potential for manipulation. While Facebook introduced privacy settings and controls, navigating the intricacies of data sharing remained a challenge for many users.

The pitfalls of data privacy reached a climax with scandals such as the Cambridge Analytica controversy, revealing the extent to which user data could be exploited for political purposes. The incident ignited conversations about the balance between personalization and privacy, prompting calls for increased regulation and a reevaluation of the power that platforms like Facebook wield.

The Dark Underbelly

As Facebook's user base expanded, so did instances of online bullying and harassment. The virtual realm provided a breeding ground for hate speech, cyberbullying, and trolling. The anonymity granted by the internet emboldened individuals to engage in harmful behavior that they might not engage in face-to-face.

The platform's efforts to combat online harassment have been met with mixed success. While tools were developed to report and block abusive accounts, the sheer scale of the platform made complete eradication of such behavior challenging. The consequences of unchecked harassment highlighted the urgent need to strike a balance between free expression and safeguarding users from harm.

Fostering Community

Facebook Groups emerged as hubs of shared interests, bringing together individuals from diverse backgrounds to connect over hobbies, causes, and passions. These groups fostered a sense of belonging and provided a space for individuals to seek support, share experiences, and engage in meaningful discussions.

However, the open nature of Groups also led to the formation of echo chambers and bubbles, where like-minded individuals reinforced each other's beliefs without exposure to differing perspectives. The algorithmic recommendation of Groups sometimes amplified extremist views, underscoring the challenge of maintaining healthy and inclusive online communities.

From Virtual to Real-World Impact

Facebook's role extended beyond the digital realm during times of crisis. Natural disasters, social upheavals, and emergencies prompted the platform to activate safety check features and donation tools, enabling users to contribute to relief efforts and support affected communities. The power of Facebook's user base was harnessed to make a tangible difference in the real world.

Yet, the platform's involvement in crisis response also faced scrutiny. Misinformation and fake news could spread rapidly during emergencies, highlighting the fine line between providing a platform for support and inadvertently contributing to chaos. The challenge lies in harnessing the power of collective action while ensuring the accuracy and reliability of information shared.

Conclusion

Facebook's journey from a college dorm project to a global powerhouse has been marked by remarkable advancements and complex challenges. Its social impact is a tapestry woven from threads of connection, empowerment, redefined norms, and ethical dilemmas. As we navigate the powers and pitfalls of Facebook, it becomes evident that our relationship with this digital giant is a reflection of the broader societal changes brought about by the digital age. The evolution of Facebook continues to shape and reshape the way we interact, communicate, and define our place in the ever-expanding virtual landscape.

Introduction

In an era defined by digital connectivity, social media platforms have emerged as influential players in shaping political discourse. Among these platforms, Facebook stands as a dominant force, exerting a profound impact on the way political communication unfolds and resonates globally. As we delve into the intricate tapestry of Facebook's role within the context of political discourse, it becomes evident that its influence spans diverse realms – from campaign strategies and voter engagement to polarization dynamics and the dissemination of misinformation. This article navigates through the multifaceted landscape of Facebook's involvement in political discourse, examining its implications and potential pitfalls.

The Digital Public Square

The evolution of Facebook into a virtual public square has fundamentally transformed the manner in which political actors engage with the masses. Gone are the days of conventional campaign strategies; the digital era has ushered in a new era of direct voter engagement, where politicians and campaigners harness the power of social media to interact with citizens in real time. With features like live videos and interactive posts, Facebook has become a platform that fosters genuine conversations between candidates and voters, eliminating intermediaries and enabling authentic connections.

Intriguingly, micro-targeting has emerged as a cornerstone of modern political campaigns, with Facebook providing a fertile ground for tailoring messages to specific demographics. By analyzing user data and preferences, campaigns can craft narratives that resonate deeply with particular voter groups, effectively personalizing their outreach strategies. This ability to speak directly to the hearts and minds of voters enhances the efficiency and impact of political messaging, making it an invaluable tool in the arsenal of modern campaigns.

At the heart of this transformation lies the phenomenon of viral campaigns. The viral nature of content sharing on Facebook can lead to rapid and widespread dissemination of political messages. Cleverly crafted posts, videos, and memes can go viral within hours, capturing the attention of millions and altering the course of political discourse. The sheer velocity and reach of viral campaigns demonstrate Facebook's role as an amplifier, where grassroots movements and political causes can gain unprecedented traction.

Polarization and Echo Chambers

While Facebook's ability to amplify voices and facilitate dialogue is undeniable, it has not been without its share of criticisms. One of the most concerning issues is the platform's potential to contribute to political polarization and the creation of echo chambers. As algorithms curate content based on user preferences, they inadvertently reinforce existing beliefs and limit exposure to diverse viewpoints.

Filter bubbles, a byproduct of algorithmic personalization, have become an inescapable part of the digital landscape. Users find themselves immersed in an online environment where their pre-existing beliefs are echoed and amplified, while dissenting opinions remain largely absent. This phenomenon, often driven by confirmation bias, can deepen societal divides and hinder productive discourse.

Yet, Facebook's paradoxical nature also offers a glimmer of hope in bridging these divides. Online communities, such as Facebook Groups, have emerged as spaces where individuals with shared interests, including political affiliations, can gather and engage in constructive discussions. These groups provide a platform for deliberative discourse, enabling users to explore differing perspectives in a respectful manner. By fostering a sense of community, Facebook has inadvertently created opportunities for users to break free from their echo chambers and engage in meaningful exchange.

Misinformation and Disinformation

The rise of fake news within the digital sphere has amplified concerns about the role of Facebook in influencing public opinion and democratic processes. The speed at which misinformation spreads on the platform, coupled with its massive user base, has the potential to sway elections, shape policy decisions, and erode the fabric of informed democracy.

Clickbait and sensationalism, often used as vehicles for fake news, tap into human emotions to generate engagement and shares. This has given rise to a climate where sensational yet inaccurate stories thrive, capturing the attention of unsuspecting users and perpetuating false narratives. The implications are profound, as misinformation can lead to misguided public sentiments and, in extreme cases, even contribute to social unrest.

Foreign interference is another troubling aspect of Facebook's role in political discourse. The platform has been exploited by state and non-state actors to disseminate disinformation campaigns aimed at influencing elections and sowing discord. High-profile instances of such interference have highlighted the challenges in safeguarding democratic processes in the digital age.

In response, efforts have been made to combat misinformation through fact-checking initiatives and content moderation. Collaborations with third-party fact-checkers aim to identify and flag false information, reducing its virality. However, the delicate balance between preserving free speech and addressing harmful content remains an ongoing challenge.

Regulatory Efforts and Ethical Dilemmas

The unprecedented influence of Facebook in shaping political discourse has prompted discussions about the need for increased regulation and ethical considerations. Striking a balance between upholding principles of free speech, ensuring user privacy, and managing content responsibly presents complex challenges that resonate beyond the platform itself.

The Cambridge Analytica scandal serves as a stark reminder of the potential consequences of lax data privacy practices. The misuse of user data for political purposes unveiled the vulnerabilities inherent in the digital landscape. As political campaigns become increasingly data-driven, questions arise about the ethical implications of harnessing user information for strategic gain.

Section 230 is a provision in the U.S. Communications Decency Act that grants online platforms legal immunity from being held liable for the content posted by their users, while also allowing them to moderate or remove objectionable content without losing this immunity. The concept of Section 230, which grants tech platforms immunity from liability for user-generated content, has also come under scrutiny. While this provision has enabled online spaces for open discourse, it raises questions about accountability when platforms are used to spread harmful or false information. The debate over censorship versus moderation further accentuates the ethical tightrope that Facebook and other platforms must navigate.

Conclusion

Facebook's role in political discourse is emblematic of the complex interplay between technological innovation, societal dynamics, and democratic values. Its evolution from a social networking site to a digital public square has revolutionized political communication, amplifying voices and enabling direct engagement. However, the platform's influence is accompanied by a set of challenges, including polarization dynamics, the spread of misinformation, and the ethical responsibilities of content moderation.

As societies grapple with these complexities, it becomes evident that harnessing the power of Facebook and similar platforms requires a concerted effort from stakeholders across the spectrum. Policymakers, tech companies, civil society, and individual users must collaborate to strike a delicate balance between enabling democratic discourse and mitigating the potential pitfalls. By acknowledging the multifaceted role of Facebook in political discourse, we can chart a path towards a more informed, engaged, and resilient democratic landscape.

Chapter 18. Twitter's Role in Activism and Social Movements

Introduction

In today's interconnected digital age, social media platforms have emerged as powerful tools that shape the landscape of activism and social movements. Among these platforms, Twitter stands out as a unique and influential platform that has played a pivotal role in catalyzing, spreading, and sustaining various social and political movements around the world. From the #ArabSpring to #BlackLivesMatter, Twitter has proven itself to be a double-edged sword, offering both unprecedented opportunities for mobilization and organization, while also presenting certain pitfalls and challenges. This article delves into the powers and pitfalls of Twitter in the realm of activism and social movements, examining its impact, reach, and consequences.

The Digital Age of Activism

In the digital age, social media platforms have revolutionized the way people communicate and engage with socio-political issues. Twitter, with its unique microblogging format, has become a central hub for activists and organizers to amplify their voices, connect with like-minded individuals, and galvanize action. Its real-time nature, concise format, and global reach have contributed to its widespread adoption in activism.

Twitter as a Catalyst for Change

Twitter's role as a catalyst for change is evident in its ability to swiftly mobilize people around critical issues. The platform's hashtag feature has proven to be a powerful tool for starting and promoting social movements. For instance, the #ArabSpring movement, which began in 2010, saw citizens across the Middle East and North Africa use Twitter to coordinate protests, share information, and challenge oppressive regimes. The ease of sharing multimedia content, such as photos and videos, has enabled activists to document and disseminate evidence of human rights abuses, shedding light on previously hidden atrocities.

Amplification of Marginalized Voices

One of Twitter's most significant strengths is its ability to amplify marginalized voices that might otherwise go unheard. Activists from marginalized communities can leverage the platform to gain visibility and draw attention to their struggles. The #BlackLivesMatter movement, sparked by the tragic death of Trayvon Martin and later amplified by the deaths of Michael Brown and Eric Garner, gained momentum through Twitter. The platform allowed activists to share personal stories, experiences, and demands, leading to a global movement that highlights racial injustice and police brutality.

Global Connectivity and Solidarity

Twitter's global reach facilitates cross-border solidarity and collaboration among activists. Movements like #MeToo, which advocates against sexual harassment and assault, gained international traction through Twitter. Survivors and supporters from different parts of the world connected, shared stories, and exchanged resources, creating a global network of activism. This interconnectedness enables the exchange of strategies, tactics, and lessons learned, ultimately strengthening the collective impact of social movements.

Real-Time Advocacy and Rapid Response

Twitter's real-time nature has transformed it into a platform for rapid advocacy and response. Activists can quickly disseminate urgent information, rally support, and organize actions in response to emerging events. During natural disasters, humanitarian crises, or political developments, Twitter serves as a vital channel for sharing critical updates and coordinating relief efforts. This real-time advocacy has the potential to save lives and drive meaningful change in a matter of hours.

Pitfalls and Challenges of Twitter Activism

While Twitter offers numerous benefits for activism and social movements, it also presents certain pitfalls and challenges that must be acknowledged.

1. Shallow Engagement and Slacktivism

The ease of retweeting, liking, and using hashtags can lead to shallow engagement and a phenomenon known as slacktivism. Individuals may believe that their social media activity alone constitutes meaningful action, without taking tangible steps offline. While Twitter can help raise awareness, true change often requires sustained, offline efforts.

2. Echo Chambers and Polarization

Twitter's algorithmic design can create echo chambers where users are exposed primarily to viewpoints that align with their existing beliefs. This can reinforce polarization and hinder productive dialogue. Activists may find themselves in isolated digital spaces, preaching to the choir rather than engaging with diverse perspectives.

3. Misinformation and Disinformation

The rapid spread of information on Twitter can lead to the unchecked dissemination of misinformation and disinformation. During social movements, false narratives can quickly gain traction, undermining the credibility of activists and diverting attention from legitimate issues. Discerning credible sources and verifying information becomes increasingly challenging in the digital noise.

4. Performative Activism

Twitter's public nature can sometimes lead to performative activism, where individuals engage in social justice issues for appearance rather than genuine commitment. This can dilute the authenticity of movements and distract from meaningful progress.

Navigating the Twitterverse

Effectively leveraging Twitter for activism requires a thoughtful approach and strategic considerations.

1. Building Authenticity and Credibility

To counter performative activism, activists should prioritize authenticity and credibility. Sharing personal experiences, reliable sources, and actionable information can establish trust and legitimacy.

2. Fostering Dialogue and Inclusivity

To address echo chambers, activists must actively seek out diverse perspectives and engage in constructive dialogue. Inclusivity can broaden the movement's reach and encourage meaningful exchange.

3. Verifying Information and Combating Misinformation

Combatting misinformation requires vigilance. Activists can play a role by fact-checking, referencing reliable sources, and encouraging critical thinking among their followers.

4. Balancing Online and Offline Action

While Twitter is a powerful tool, it should complement, not replace, offline action. Activists must strike a balance between online advocacy and tangible efforts on the ground.

The Future of Twitter in Activism

As Twitter continues to evolve, its role in activism and social movements will likely evolve as well. Activists must remain adaptable and creative, harnessing the platform's strengths while navigating its pitfalls.

1. Leveraging Emerging Features

Activists can explore and adapt to new Twitter features, such as audio and video tweets or Spaces, to engage with audiences in innovative ways.

2. Collaborative Campaigns

Collaborative campaigns that unite activists from different platforms can amplify messages and mobilize broader audiences.

3. Ethical Considerations

As activism on Twitter grows, ethical considerations become paramount. Activists must be transparent, respectful of privacy, and mindful of the potential consequences of their online actions.

Conclusion

Twitter's role in activism and social movements is both transformative and complex. It has empowered marginalized voices, facilitated global solidarity, and ignited change. However, its potential for performative activism, polarization, and misinformation must be acknowledged and addressed. By understanding and navigating these powers and pitfalls, activists can harness Twitter's influence to drive meaningful, lasting change in the world.

In the ever-evolving landscape of social media, Twitter stands as a testament to the interconnectedness of our world and the potential for digital platforms to serve as catalysts for social progress. As activists continue to wield the power of Twitter, they must remain vigilant, creative, and committed to making the most of this powerful tool in their ongoing pursuit of justice and change.

Introduction

In today's interconnected and digitally-driven world, social media platforms have revolutionized the way people communicate and interact. The emergence of platforms like Facebook, Twitter, and Instagram has not only transformed personal connections but has also extended its reach to the realm of international relations. This article delves into the concept of "Twitter diplomacy" and explores the multifaceted role that social media, particularly Twitter, plays in shaping and influencing international relations.

The Rise of Social Media Diplomacy

Traditional diplomacy, characterized by closed-door negotiations and official channels, has gradually found itself complemented and, at times, challenged by the rise of social media. Social media platforms have provided a unique platform for political leaders, diplomats, governments, and international organizations to engage with a global audience instantaneously. Among these platforms, Twitter stands out as a prominent player, enabling what has come to be known as "Twitter diplomacy."

Instantaneous Global Reach

One of the most significant advantages of Twitter diplomacy is its ability to provide instantaneous global reach. Diplomats and world leaders can communicate directly with each other and with the public, bypassing traditional media gatekeepers. This direct interaction allows for real-time responses to emerging issues, crises, or events, fostering a sense of transparency and accessibility. Whether it's announcing policy decisions, addressing international incidents, or expressing condolences, Twitter enables rapid dissemination of information to a worldwide audience.

Shaping Public Opinion

Twitter diplomacy extends beyond official communications between governments. It has become a powerful tool for shaping public opinion on an international scale. Leaders can use Twitter to set the narrative and influence how their actions are perceived globally. Through carefully crafted tweets, leaders can highlight their achievements, articulate policy positions, and rally public support. This ability to engage directly with citizens of other countries has the potential to bridge cultural gaps and foster a better understanding of complex geopolitical issues.

Conflict Resolution and De-Escalation

While social media can sometimes be a source of tension, it also has the potential to facilitate conflict resolution and de-escalation. Twitter diplomacy allows leaders to engage in public diplomacy, reaching out to adversaries or rivals in a less formal and confrontational manner. Publicly expressed goodwill gestures, such as congratulatory messages or expressions of sympathy during times of crisis, can contribute to reducing hostilities and creating an atmosphere conducive to dialogue.

Challenges and Pitfalls

While Twitter diplomacy offers numerous opportunities, it is not without its challenges and pitfalls. One of the primary concerns is the potential for miscommunication or misinterpretation due to the character limitations of tweets. Complex geopolitical issues often require nuanced explanations that may not fit within the constraints of a tweet, leading to oversimplification or distortion of important information.

The Risk of Diplomatic Blunders

The informality of social media can also lead to diplomatic blunders that have far-reaching consequences. A poorly worded tweet or an ill-considered response can escalate tensions or strain relations between countries. The lack of face-to-face interaction and the absence of diplomatic protocols can increase the likelihood of misunderstandings or unintended provocations.

Weaponization and Disinformation

Social media platforms, including Twitter, have been weaponized by state and non-state actors to spread disinformation and sow discord. Fake accounts, bots, and orchestrated campaigns can amplify false narratives, undermining trust and complicating diplomatic efforts. The speed at which misinformation spreads on social media makes it challenging for diplomatic channels to counteract or correct the false information effectively.

Case Studies in Twitter Diplomacy

Several case studies highlight the evolving role of Twitter diplomacy in international relations:

1. Iran Nuclear Deal

Twitter played a crucial role in shaping public opinion and garnering international support for the Iran Nuclear Deal. Diplomats from various countries, including the United States and Iran, used Twitter to explain the intricacies of the agreement and respond to criticisms, ultimately contributing to the successful negotiation of the deal.

2. North Korea-U.S. Relations

Twitter diplomacy played a role in the rollercoaster-like relationship between North Korea and the United States. Leaders from both countries engaged in a series of tweets, ranging from threatening rhetoric to moments of apparent detente. While not a substitute for traditional diplomacy, these interactions demonstrated the potential for social media to influence diplomatic dynamics.

3. Vaccine Diplomacy

The COVID-19 pandemic witnessed the emergence of vaccine diplomacy, where countries used social media, including Twitter, to showcase their efforts in providing vaccines to other nations. This digital diplomacy allowed countries to project a positive image and gain international recognition for their contributions to global public health.

The Future of Twitter Diplomacy

As social media continues to evolve, so too will its role in international relations. The future of Twitter diplomacy will likely involve a combination of benefits and challenges:

1. Enhanced Dialogue: Twitter diplomacy could facilitate increased dialogue between governments, allowing leaders to engage in informal discussions and establish rapport that can later support formal negotiations.

2. Cybersecurity and Disinformation Countermeasures: Diplomats and governments will need to develop robust cybersecurity strategies and effective countermeasures to combat disinformation campaigns that exploit social media platforms.

3. Public Diplomacy 2.0: Public diplomacy will further evolve as leaders leverage social media to directly engage with citizens of other countries, fostering greater people-to-people connections.

4. Ethical Considerations: The ethical dimensions of Twitter diplomacy, including issues of privacy, accountability, and responsibility, will require careful consideration to ensure its responsible use.

Conclusion

The advent of Twitter diplomacy and its role in international relations highlights the dynamic interplay between technology, communication, and diplomacy. While social media platforms like Twitter offer unprecedented opportunities for engagement and transparency, they also introduce new challenges and complexities. The powers and pitfalls of Twitter diplomacy underscore the need for a thoughtful and balanced approach, where traditional diplomatic channels work in tandem with digital tools to navigate the intricacies of our interconnected world. As social media platforms continue to shape the global landscape, diplomats and leaders must adapt to harness the potential of Twitter diplomacy while mitigating its inherent risks.

Introduction

In an era of rapid digital transformation and interconnectedness, social media platforms have become pivotal players in shaping the way we consume news and information. Among these platforms, Twitter stands out as a dynamic and influential force within the contemporary news landscape. This article delves into the powers and pitfalls of Twitter as a news dissemination platform, analyzing its impact on the spread of information, its role in fostering public discourse, and the challenges it presents in maintaining journalistic integrity and combating misinformation.

The Power of the Tweet

Twitter's unique and succinct format, with its 280-character limit, has revolutionized the speed at which news travels. This brevity forces users to distill complex stories into concise snippets, making it ideal for breaking news and live event coverage. Unlike traditional news outlets, where editorial processes can delay reporting, Twitter allows real-time updates directly from the source. The platform's capacity to bypass intermediaries and facilitate direct communication between individuals and news events has redefined the relationship between journalists, newsmakers, and the audience.

However, this rapid transmission of information has its pitfalls. The race to be the first to report can sometimes lead to inaccuracies or incomplete information being shared. Missteps and errors can spread just as quickly as verified news, potentially sowing confusion and eroding trust in both traditional journalism and social media as credible sources. The pressure to generate engagement and attract followers may also incentivize sensationalism, further blurring the line between news and entertainment.

Twitter as the Public Forum

Beyond its role in disseminating news, Twitter has transformed into a virtual public square where individuals, journalists, politicians, and organizations engage in discussions on current events and social issues. The platform has democratized public discourse, providing a space for marginalized voices to be heard and for citizens to hold powerful entities accountable. Hashtags have become rallying points for social movements, allowing disparate individuals to coalesce around shared causes, transcending geographical and political boundaries.

However, this open forum also exposes users to echo chambers and filter bubbles, where they are primarily exposed to viewpoints that align with their existing beliefs. This can hinder constructive debate and contribute to polarization. Additionally, the brevity of tweets may oversimplify complex issues, stifling nuanced discussions and promoting knee-jerk reactions rather than thoughtful analysis. The lack of context and space for in-depth exploration can inadvertently contribute to a superficial understanding of complex topics.

Navigating the Misinformation Minefield

One of the most significant challenges posed by Twitter in the news landscape is the proliferation of misinformation and disinformation. The platform's speed and reach make it a fertile ground for the rapid dissemination of falsehoods, rumors, and conspiracy theories. The lack of stringent fact-checking and editorial oversight inherent in traditional journalism can contribute to the spread of inaccuracies. Furthermore, the viral nature of retweets can amplify false information to a massive audience before corrective measures can be taken.

Efforts to combat misinformation on Twitter have included algorithmic interventions, partnerships with fact-checking organizations, and user reporting mechanisms. However, striking the balance between preserving free speech and curbing the spread of false information is a complex challenge. Misinformation can also be weaponized for political purposes, raising concerns about the platform's role in influencing public opinion and electoral outcomes.

The Evolving Role of Journalists

Journalists, once the gatekeepers of information, have had to adapt to Twitter's influence on news dissemination. The platform has given journalists unprecedented access to sources and real-time updates, enabling them to break stories and engage with their audience directly. However, this shift has blurred the lines between traditional reporting and personal expression, raising questions about objectivity, editorial standards, and conflicts of interest.

While Twitter allows journalists to engage with their audience and build their personal brand, it also exposes them to harassment, trolling, and online abuse. The immediacy of Twitter can pressure journalists into hasty reporting, sacrificing accuracy for speed. Additionally, the emphasis on sensationalism and clickbait can undermine the integrity of journalism by incentivizing attention-grabbing headlines and shallow content.

Conclusion

Twitter's impact on the news landscape is undeniable, reshaping how information is disseminated, consumed, and debated. Its strengths lie in its rapidity, interactivity, and potential to amplify marginalized voices. Yet, its weaknesses – the potential for misinformation, echo chambers, and challenges to journalistic integrity – cannot be ignored.

As society grapples with the powers and pitfalls of Twitter and other social media platforms, it becomes imperative to strike a balance between harnessing the benefits of instant communication and safeguarding the principles of accuracy, fairness, and responsible journalism. Navigating the twists and turns of this dynamic landscape requires collective efforts from platforms, journalists, users, and society at large. Only through a commitment to critical thinking, media literacy, and ethical reporting can we fully harness the potential of Twitter while mitigating its pitfalls in the ever-evolving news ecosystem.

Introduction

The emergence of social media platforms such as Facebook, Twitter, and Instagram has transformed the global landscape of communication and information dissemination. These platforms have revolutionized the way people connect, share, and engage with each other. However, this revolutionary power has not come without its pitfalls. In recent years, the issue of election interference and social media manipulation has taken center stage, raising concerns about the potential for these platforms to undermine democratic processes and influence public opinion. This article delves into the complex web of election interference and social media manipulation, exploring the various facets, mechanisms, and challenges presented by this digital phenomenon.

The Rise of Social Media Manipulation

The digital era has heralded unprecedented opportunities for information dissemination, empowering individuals to engage in public discourse and participate in political conversations. Social media platforms, with their user-friendly interfaces and extensive reach, have become breeding grounds for political discussions and activism. However, this openness has also given rise to nefarious activities, including the manipulation of public opinion for political gain.

The Mechanisms of Manipulation

Social media manipulation encompasses a range of tactics employed to influence public opinion and sway electoral outcomes. One of the primary methods is the dissemination of false or misleading information. Malicious actors create and spread fabricated stories, photos, and videos that cater to pre-existing biases, exploiting emotional triggers to garner engagement and virality. This information can then go viral, leading to the amplification of falsehoods and the distortion of public discourse.

Additionally, the use of fake accounts and bots plays a pivotal role in social media manipulation. These automated accounts can rapidly disseminate content, manipulate trending topics, and simulate organic engagement, creating the illusion of widespread support or opposition. Such tactics not only distort public sentiment but also make it difficult to discern authentic voices from orchestrated campaigns.

Targeted Advertising and Micro-Targeting

Another potent tool in the arsenal of social media manipulation is targeted advertising and micro-targeting. By harnessing the vast data accumulated from users' online activities, advertisers can craft tailored messages that resonate with specific demographic groups. While this can be a legitimate marketing strategy, it becomes problematic when employed for political purposes. Micro-targeting allows political campaigns to deliver personalized messages, often exploiting users' vulnerabilities and influencing their decision-making processes.

The Specter of Election Interference

Election interference refers to deliberate efforts by foreign entities or domestic actors to undermine the integrity of electoral processes in other countries. Social media platforms have emerged as favored battlegrounds for these operations due to their ability to disseminate information quickly and widely. Foreign actors can exploit existing divisions within a society, exacerbating tensions and sowing discord to weaken democratic institutions.

Case Studies in Interference

Several high-profile cases of election interference through social media manipulation have garnered international attention. The 2016 United States presidential election stands as a watershed moment, with evidence indicating that Russian operatives utilized platforms like Facebook and Twitter to disseminate divisive content and sow confusion among American voters. Similarly, allegations of foreign interference have surfaced in elections across Europe, illustrating the global nature of this challenge.

Countering Manipulation

Addressing the complex issue of election interference and social media manipulation demands a multi-pronged approach. Platforms themselves bear a significant responsibility in combating these threats. Increased transparency regarding political advertising and the identification of automated accounts are steps in the right direction. However, striking a balance between curbing manipulation and preserving free speech remains a formidable challenge.

Collaboration between governments, technology companies, and civil society is vital. Legislation and regulations must be developed to hold malicious actors accountable while safeguarding users' rights. Additionally, media literacy programs can empower users to critically evaluate information, fortifying them against manipulation.

The Ethical Quandary

The powers of social media platforms extend beyond mere technological capabilities; they delve into ethical and moral dimensions. These platforms wield immense influence over public opinion, which raises questions about their ethical responsibilities. Should these platforms be neutral conduits for information, or do they bear a duty to curtail the spread of misinformation and manipulation, even at the cost of limiting certain forms of expression?

Looking Ahead

As technology continues to evolve, so do the methods and techniques of election interference and social media manipulation. Deepfake technology, artificial intelligence, and advanced algorithms could potentially amplify these challenges, making the task of identifying and countering manipulation even more daunting. Deepfake technology is artificial intelligence (AI) or machine learning-based techniques used to create highly realistic and often convincing manipulated audio, video, or images that depict events or actions that never occurred, often raising ethical and privacy concerns due to their potential for misinformation and deception.

To harness the potential of social media platforms while mitigating their pitfalls, a collaborative effort is required. The powers of Facebook, Twitter, and Instagram, when harnessed responsibly, can serve as tools for fostering democratic engagement, facilitating constructive conversations, and promoting social progress. However, without effective safeguards and collective action, these platforms could continue to be vulnerable to exploitation, undermining the very foundations of democratic societies.

Conclusion

The powers and pitfalls of Facebook, Twitter, and Instagram are inextricably linked to the challenge of election interference and social media manipulation. These platforms have demonstrated their ability to unite voices, ignite movements, and drive social change. Simultaneously, they have been leveraged to spread falsehoods, amplify divisions, and undermine democratic processes. The complex interplay between technological innovation, political manipulation, and ethical considerations underscores the need for a comprehensive and coordinated response. As societies grapple with this digital conundrum, a delicate balance must be struck between preserving freedom of expression and safeguarding the integrity of democratic discourse. Only through concerted efforts can we hope to navigate the treacherous waters of election interference and social media manipulation, ensuring that the promise of digital connectivity is not eclipsed by its potential pitfalls.

Introduction

In the ever-evolving landscape of social media, platforms like Facebook, Twitter, and Instagram have given rise to a new phenomenon known as the "Influencer Economy." This digital era has witnessed the emergence of individuals who wield significant influence over their followers, thanks to their curated online personas and engaging content. This article delves into the intricacies of the Influencer Economy, exploring its successes, struggles, and the critical aspect of sustainability that underpins this contemporary phenomenon.

The Rise of the Influencer Economy

1. The Birth of Social Media Stars

The Influencer Economy owes its origins to the democratization of content creation facilitated by platforms like Facebook, Twitter, and Instagram. Ordinary individuals gained the ability to share their lives, insights, and expertise, thereby attracting a devoted following.

2. The Power of Authenticity

Unlike traditional celebrities, influencers have built their fame on authenticity. By sharing relatable stories and engaging in genuine interactions with their audience, influencers foster a sense of connection that resonates deeply.

Successes in the Influencer Economy

1. Monetization and Financial Rewards

The Earning Potential: Influencers have transformed their online presence into lucrative careers. By partnering with brands for sponsored content, affiliate marketing, and product collaborations, they harness their influence to generate substantial income.

Diversification of Revenue Streams: Many influencers have expanded beyond brand partnerships, leveraging their popularity to launch their products, merchandise, or digital content. This diversification bolsters their financial stability and offers a buffer against platform changes.

2. Niche Communities and Cultural Impact

Fostering Niche Communities: Influencers often cater to specific interests, allowing them to cultivate tight-knit communities centered around shared passions. These communities provide a safe space for enthusiasts to connect and engage.

Driving Cultural Trends: Influencers wield the power to shape cultural norms and influence trends. From fashion and beauty to social and political issues, their voices contribute to the shaping of public discourse.

Struggles in the Influencer Economy

1. Authenticity vs. Commercialization

Balancing Authenticity: The pressure to monetize can strain the authenticity that initially garnered an influencer's following. Striking a balance between commercial opportunities and genuine content becomes a delicate challenge.

Loss of Credibility: Over-commercialization can lead to a loss of credibility as followers may perceive influencers as mere promoters, eroding the trust that is crucial for sustainable success.

2. Mental Health and Burnout

Constant Visibility: Influencers are under constant scrutiny, leading to heightened stress and anxiety. The need to maintain a flawless image can take a toll on their mental well-being.

Unpredictable Income: The instability of influencer income, often reliant on collaborations and partnerships, can cause financial stress and uncertainty, exacerbating mental health challenges.

Sustainability in the Influencer Economy

1. Longevity Through Adaptability

Adapting to Platform Changes: In an ever-changing digital landscape, influencers who successfully adapt to algorithm shifts and new platform features are better poised for long-term success.

Investing in Skill Development: Influencers who invest in honing their skills, whether in content creation, digital marketing, or business management, can pivot and explore diverse opportunities beyond the influencer role.

2. Fostering Genuine Connections

Prioritizing Community Building: Sustainable influencers prioritize fostering genuine connections with their followers, valuing quality interactions over vanity metrics like follower count.

Openness About Struggles: Influencers who share their challenges, setbacks, and personal growth stories not only humanize themselves but also create a supportive environment that resonates with their audience.

The Future of the Influencer Economy

Continued Evolution: As social media platforms evolve, the Influencer Economy will continue to adapt, giving rise to new formats, trends, and opportunities for content creators.

Diversification and Specialization: Future influencers might focus on micro-niches or specific demographics, fostering even deeper connections with their followers.

Conclusion

The Influencer Economy, driven by the powers of Facebook, Twitter, and Instagram, stands as a testament to the digital age's transformative potential. While it celebrates the successes and achievements of influencers, it also highlights the struggles they face in an ever-changing landscape. Sustainability in this economy hinges on the ability to strike a delicate balance between authenticity, commercialization, mental well-being, and adaptability. As we peer into the future, the Influencer Economy will undoubtedly continue to shape our online interactions, cultural trends, and the very nature of fame itself.

Introduction

In the ever-evolving landscape of social media, Instagram has emerged as a powerful force, shaping cultural trends and driving globalization in ways that were once unimaginable. This platform, primarily focused on visual content, has transcended its origins as a mere photo-sharing app to become a catalyst for societal shifts and cross-cultural exchanges. As we delve into the powers and pitfalls of Instagram within the context of the broader social media sphere, we uncover its profound impact on shaping cultural narratives and propelling the forces of globalization.

The Rise of Instagram and Its Cultural Significance

The inception of Instagram in 2010 marked a paradigm shift in how individuals engage with visual content and connect with the world around them. Unlike its textual counterparts, such as Facebook and Twitter, Instagram's emphasis on images and videos allowed users to share their stories and experiences in a more immersive and immediate manner. This unique approach to communication not only transformed the way people interacted online but also laid the foundation for Instagram's role as a global cultural influencer.

Visual Storytelling

At the heart of Instagram's impact on cultural trends lies its role as a platform for visual storytelling. Through curated posts and meticulously crafted aesthetics, users have harnessed the power of images to communicate their identities, experiences, and beliefs. Influencers, artists, and everyday individuals alike have turned their profiles into virtual galleries, sharing not only their daily lives but also propagating trends and ideals.

This visual language transcends linguistic barriers, enabling cross-cultural connections that were once hindered by differences in language and communication styles. A photograph taken in a bustling Tokyo street can resonate with someone in New York, evoking a shared sense of wanderlust and appreciation for urban beauty. In this manner, Instagram serves as a bridge between cultures, allowing individuals to learn, empathize, and celebrate the diversity of the global community.

Hashtags and Virality

One of Instagram's most potent tools for shaping cultural trends is the hashtag. The unassuming '#' symbol has evolved into a formidable force, capable of catapulting ideas, movements, and challenges into the global spotlight. Through the strategic use of hashtags, users can categorize their content and participate in broader conversations, contributing to the propagation of cultural phenomena.

The ALS Ice Bucket Challenge was a viral social media campaign that aimed to raise awareness and funds for amyotrophic lateral sclerosis (ALS), also known as Lou Gehrig's disease. The ALS Ice Bucket Challenge serves as a prime example of Instagram's ability to facilitate viral trends. What started as a grassroots movement to raise awareness about ALS quickly snowballed into a worldwide sensation, with individuals from all corners of the globe taking part and nominating others. This chain reaction showcased how Instagram's network effect can amplify messages and drive collective action, transcending geographic and cultural boundaries.

Cultural Appropriation vs. Appreciation

While Instagram has undoubtedly fostered cultural exchange, it has also brought to light complex issues surrounding cultural appropriation and appreciation. The platform's democratized nature allows users to engage with and adopt elements of different cultures, often blurring the line between genuine appreciation and shallow mimicry.

Fashion trends, for instance, can spread rapidly across continents, exposing users to diverse styles and aesthetics. Yet, the line between embracing cultural diversity and exploiting it can be thin. The debate over appropriative Halloween costumes or the use of sacred symbols as mere fashion statements illustrates the challenges that arise when cultural elements are divorced from their original context. Instagram's role in both facilitating cross-cultural exchange and inadvertently perpetuating cultural insensitivity underscores the need for users to approach cultural borrowing with sensitivity and respect.

Influencers as Cultural Aggregators

Instagram influencers have emerged as modern-day cultural intermediaries, wielding significant influence over their followers' perceptions of beauty, lifestyle, and societal norms. These digital tastemakers curate and project aspirational lifestyles, shaping cultural ideals and fostering a sense of belonging among their audiences.

The beauty industry offers a compelling case study. Influencers, armed with an arsenal of filters and editing tools, often project an unrealistic standard of beauty that can have far-reaching effects on individuals' self-esteem and self-worth. The "Instagram face," characterized by flawless skin, contoured features, and full lips, has become a global phenomenon, driving cosmetic procedures and altering cultural perceptions of beauty. While influencers have the power to challenge traditional norms and promote body positivity, they also bear the responsibility of promoting authentic representations and ethical practices.

Globalization Redefined

Instagram's impact on globalization extends beyond the dissemination of cultural trends; it has redefined the concept of global communities. While physical distance still separates individuals, the platform's interconnectedness has fostered a sense of shared experiences and collective consciousness.

Virtual events, live streams, and IGTV have enabled users to participate in global conversations in real time. From climate change rallies to cultural festivals, Instagram has democratized access to events that were once limited by geographic constraints. This transformation of how individuals engage with global issues underscores the platform's potential to inspire real-world action and social change.

The Dark Side

As we explore the powers and pitfalls of Instagram's influence on cultural trends and globalization, it is crucial to acknowledge its role in fostering negative psychological and societal consequences. The platform's emphasis on image crafting and validation can breed narcissistic tendencies, where self-worth becomes contingent on likes and followers. The incessant pursuit of the perfect post can detract from genuine experiences and authentic connections, perpetuating a cycle of insecurity and dissatisfaction.

Additionally, the fear of missing out (FOMO) has been amplified by Instagram's curated content. Users often perceive others' lives as more exciting and fulfilling, leading to feelings of inadequacy and isolation. The paradoxical nature of a platform designed to connect individuals potentially exacerbates loneliness and disconnection, underscoring the need for users to strike a balance between virtual and real-life interactions.

Conclusion

Instagram's profound impact on cultural trends and globalization is undeniable. From its origins as a visual storytelling platform to its role as a global cultural influencer, Instagram has reshaped how we communicate, connect, and perceive the world around us. The platform's ability to facilitate cross-cultural exchange, amplify trends, and redefine global communities has transformed the social media landscape.

However, as we navigate the cultural currents shaped by Instagram, it is imperative to remain mindful of its potential pitfalls. Balancing the pursuit of validation with genuine self-expression, navigating the fine line between appreciation and appropriation, and fostering meaningful connections amidst the curated content are all essential considerations.

Ultimately, Instagram's powers and pitfalls within the realm of cultural trends and globalization remind us that while it holds the potential to unite and inspire, our usage must be guided by intention, empathy, and a nuanced understanding of the diverse and interconnected world we inhabit.

Introduction

In recent years, the rise of social media platforms such as Facebook, Twitter, and Instagram has transformed the way people communicate, share information, and engage with the world. These platforms have provided unprecedented opportunities for connectivity, self-expression, and business growth. However, with great power comes great responsibility, and the unregulated nature of social media has given rise to a myriad of challenges ranging from misinformation and privacy concerns to cyberbullying and political manipulation. As these platforms continue to shape the fabric of modern society, there is an urgent need for effective regulation to address these issues and ensure a safer and more transparent digital landscape.

The Evolution of Social Media and Its Impact

Social media platforms emerged as virtual spaces where individuals could connect, share content, and interact with a global audience. The rapid growth of platforms like Facebook, Twitter, and Instagram has played a pivotal role in reshaping communication dynamics, empowering marginalized voices, and fostering a new era of digital activism. These platforms have become essential tools for political mobilization, social awareness campaigns, and business promotion. However, their unbridled growth has also led to the proliferation of harmful content, including hate speech, fake news, and cyberbullying.

The Need for Regulation

The immense influence wielded by social media platforms necessitates a comprehensive regulatory framework that balances innovation with accountability. While these platforms champion free speech and open dialogue, the absence of effective regulation has enabled the spread of disinformation, manipulation, and harassment. Regulation should aim to protect users from online harm, safeguard privacy, and ensure the integrity of information shared on these platforms.

Current Regulatory Efforts

Several countries have taken steps to regulate social media platforms, each adopting a unique approach. The European Union's General Data Protection Regulation (GDPR) stands as a landmark example, emphasizing data protection, user consent, and the right to be forgotten. In the United States, the debate over Section 230 of the Communications Decency Act has intensified, with discussions centered around platforms' liability for user-generated content. Additionally, countries like Australia and India have proposed laws to curb the spread of fake news and harmful content.

Challenges in Regulating Social Media

Crafting effective regulations for social media is not without its challenges. The global nature of these platforms demands a coordinated effort among nations, as the internet transcends borders. Striking a balance between regulating harmful content and upholding free speech is a delicate task, with concerns about potential censorship and stifling innovation. Moreover, the fast-paced nature of technological advancements often outpaces the development of regulatory frameworks, leaving gaps that can be exploited.

Transparency and Accountability

One of the key pillars of effective regulation is ensuring transparency and accountability from social media platforms. Companies should be compelled to disclose their algorithms and content moderation practices to allow for independent scrutiny. Transparency reports, detailing the removal of content and enforcement of community guidelines, provide insight into platform actions. Furthermore, establishing clear mechanisms for users to appeal content decisions and report abuse is essential.

Combatting Misinformation

The rampant spread of misinformation and fake news on social media has far-reaching consequences. Regulatory efforts must focus on curbing the dissemination of false information without infringing upon legitimate expression. Fact-checking mechanisms, warning labels on dubious content, and algorithmic adjustments can help limit the virality of misinformation. Collaborative efforts between platforms, fact-checkers, and researchers can contribute to a more accurate information ecosystem.

Protecting User Privacy

The collection and utilization of user data by social media platforms have raised significant privacy concerns. Regulations should ensure that users have granular control over their data, the ability to opt out of data collection, and a clear understanding of how their information is being used. Stricter rules for obtaining user consent, data encryption, and regular audits of data handling practices can bolster user privacy.

Addressing Online Harassment

Cyberbullying and online harassment have emerged as pressing issues, particularly affecting vulnerable groups. Regulatory frameworks should establish mechanisms to swiftly address and prevent such behavior, including stronger reporting systems, content removal procedures, and collaboration with law enforcement when necessary. Creating a safer online environment requires proactive measures to deter and penalize harassers.

Election Integrity and Political Manipulation

The role of social media in influencing elections and political discourse has come under intense scrutiny. Regulations should mandate transparency in political advertising, ensuring that users can easily identify sponsored content. Efforts to combat foreign interference, fake accounts, and algorithmic manipulation are crucial to safeguarding the integrity of democratic processes.

Emerging Technologies and Future Challenges

As social media continues to evolve, new technologies like artificial intelligence, virtual reality, and augmented reality will shape the digital landscape in unforeseen ways. These innovations offer exciting possibilities for communication and engagement, but they also present novel challenges. Deepfakes, AI-generated content, and algorithmic biases raise questions about authenticity, accountability, and the potential for manipulation. Regulatory frameworks must be adaptable to these changes while upholding core principles.

Global Collaboration and Multi-Stakeholder Engagement

Given the global nature of social media platforms, effective regulation requires international collaboration and engagement among multiple stakeholders. Governments, tech companies, civil society organizations, academia, and users must come together to develop comprehensive solutions that address the complex challenges posed by social media. The creation of platforms for dialogue, knowledge sharing, and best practice exchange can facilitate a holistic approach to regulation.

Conclusion

The powers and pitfalls of social media platforms like Facebook, Twitter, and Instagram have reshaped the way we communicate, connect, and engage with information. While these platforms offer immense opportunities for positive change, their unchecked growth has also given rise to a host of challenges that demand effective regulation. Striking the right balance between free expression and responsible oversight is a complex task, but it is essential to ensure a digital landscape that is safe, transparent, and conducive to meaningful interactions. As technology continues to advance and societal norms shift, the ongoing evolution of social media regulation will remain a critical endeavor. Only through proactive, adaptive, and collaborative efforts can we navigate the intricate web of issues surrounding social media and harness its potential for the betterment of society.

This comprehensive book on "Powers and Pitfalls of Facebook, Twitter, and Instagram" delves into the captivating world of social media platforms that have transformed modern communication. Through its meticulously crafted chapters, readers embark on a journey tracing the origins and evolution of these platforms, from the rise of social media as a cultural phenomenon to the emergence of Facebook, Twitter, and Instagram as dominant players. Each chapter illuminates the unique dynamics of these platforms, from algorithmic influences shaping user experiences to the pressing concerns of privacy, content moderation, and the spread of disinformation. Engaging with the darker aspects, the book navigates through challenges such as fake news, online harassment, and cancel culture, offering insightful analyses of their impact on free speech and public discourse.

Furthermore, the book examines the transformative role of Instagram influencers, the platform's intricate relationship with mental health and body image, and its far-reaching influence on cultural trends. Noteworthy is the exploration of Facebook's and Twitter's roles in political discourse, activism, and global diplomacy, along with the intriguing interplay between these platforms and the news landscape. Concluding with a forward-looking perspective, the book contemplates the intricate task of regulating social media, paving the way for a better understanding of the complex tapestry that Facebook, Twitter, and Instagram have woven into our lives.

ABOUT THE AUTHOR

Mr. C. P. Kumar is a retired Scientist 'G' from National Institute of Hydrology, Roorkee, Uttarakhand, India. He is also a Reiki Healer and Chakra Balancing practitioner (with pendulum dowsing) and offers Emotional Freedom Technique (EFT) to help individuals with emotional issues. Mr. Kumar has authored many books on technical, spiritual, and social topics.

For further details, you may visit his webpage
https://www.angelfire.com/nh/cpkumar/virgo.html